To Pat.

Harvest

Recipes from an Organic Farm

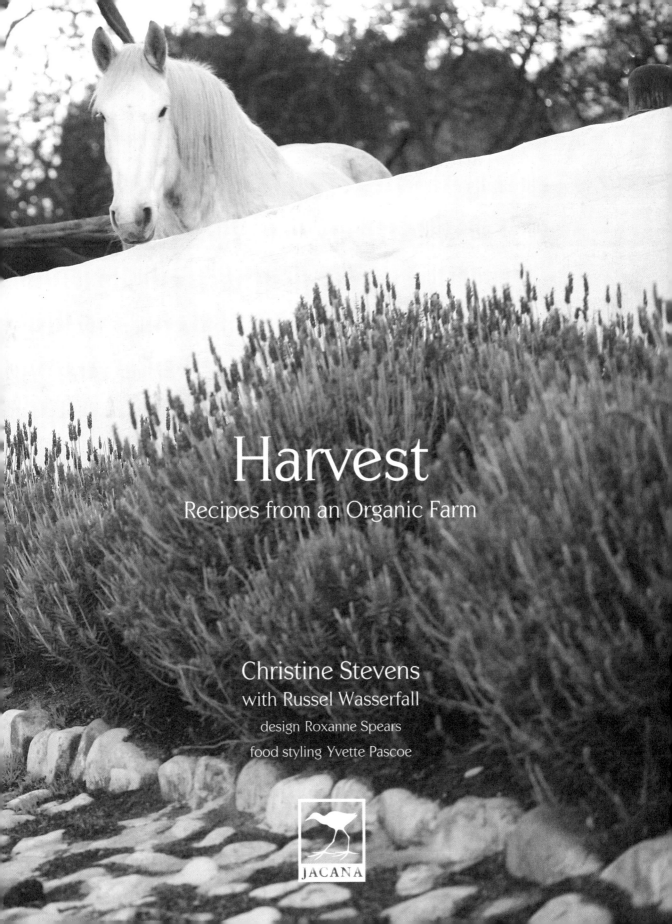

Harvest

Recipes from an Organic Farm

Christine Stevens
with Russel Wasserfall

design Roxanne Spears
food styling Yvette Pascoe

JACANA

Foreword

The Stevens' farm has to be one of the most beautiful South African farms I have ever had the privilege of visiting. Everywhere you look there's a postcard view, and everything on the land, from vines to children, is in rude good health. I first met the Stevens family in the winter of 2006, looking for a story on their monthly organic market for a local magazine. This hale family had done what so many of us dream of, leaving the city behind and carving out an enviable life on an organic farm.

With all the amazing produce heaped on tables and hanging from trees and vines, conversations with Christine turned almost immediately to food and inevitably to the organic wine which they produce under the Mountain Oaks label. It was while we were well into a few bottles of Chenin Blanc around their lunch table, with its view over the Slanghoek River Valley, that the idea for this book was born. I was amazed by Christine's incredible ability to pop out into the garden, gather some of this and a little of that and turn it into delicious meals in no time at all. There was no fuss or clatter, just a talented cook with an intimate knowledge of her ingredients from seed to pot.

The thought had barely formed before recipes were being sorted and Christine had things ready to go. She is an incredible woman of boundless energy, and I and my wine collection are happy to call her a friend. This book is a tribute to her commitment to the health of her family and the land on which they grow.

Russel Wasserfall

First published by Jacana Media (Pty) Ltd in 2008

10 Orange Street, Sunnyside, Auckland Park 2092, South Africa

+27 11 628 3200, www.jacana.co.za

ISBN 978-1-77009-594-6

Design and layout by Roxanne Spears

Printed by Craftprint, Singapore

1st edition 2008

Reprinted 2010

Job no. 001158

See a complete list of Jacana titles at www.jacana.co.za

Contents

Introduction

We settled on our farm in 2001, and if the choice of the word 'settled' to describe our arrival here seems a little dramatic, that is because it was a move that has changed our lives fundamentally. There is a sense of permanence about our being here, a sense of being completely 'settled' that feels as if we are truly part of the farm like the old almond trees or the ancient vines we found here when we arrived.

The old farmhouse was in a bad state but we loved it from the moment we first saw it. This bond easily endured the initial six weeks when we had to bathe in the river because there was no running water indoors. Beyond the big old doors, the farm rolled off across the Slanghoek River to the foot of the mountains. Had we not been ready to commit to environmentally sound farming methods and an organic lifestyle

before we arrived, that view would have been enough to set our feet on this path. Slanghoek valley was one of the earliest areas farmed by colonists moving out from the settlement at Cape Town and looking for new horizons. For us, moving here from the comfort of suburban Cape Town and the corporate world was a step into the unknown too, but we have come to see it as the best move of our lives.

Part of that unknown was wondering whether we could sustain our dream lifestyle by making the farm completely productive and profitable. Even though I had always grown vegetables and herbs for my own use in little backyard patches or ambitious window boxes, making a farm productive was another matter entirely. I've been passionate about food for as long as I can remember, and cooked since I was a child.

Because I believe fresh ingredients to be the core of good food, it was a priority for Mark and me to get a vegetable garden up and running. Two elements came into play here: self-sufficiency, and the robust good health that our family could enjoy if we managed to grow our own organic produce.

Of course, when we were sitting planning and scheming about all this, the dream included slow cooking and long, lazy lunches with loads of good friends and fantastic wine from our own grapes. It was not long before reality took a great big bite out of our plans. The truth is that it might look romantic from the outside, but farming for real is an incredible challenge on every level. You might flop into bed at the end of a long harvest day completely exhausted, only to be woken up at midnight by a neighbour because your bull has wandered onto his land or there's a fire. This is truly a labour of love, and when you let go of the sense of time and deadline that pervades city life and start working to the more natural rhythms of season and vine and people, you start to find that certain things just go a little more smoothly.

I had no choice but to learn this lesson very quickly. When we were first moving in, tragedy struck, and our farm manager was killed in an accident returning from a soccer match. My husband was still away on week days running his business, so that left me to handle the farm. Overnight I learned how to drive a forklift and a tractor. It had to be the middle of harvest, so I was up at five to get things going before waking and feeding my children to send them off to school. No sooner had the grapes come in and

the first crop was fermenting than the citrus was ripe and ready to be harvested.

At weekends, Mark used to arrive home to his exhausted wife and a list of things needing to be fixed. We were adamant that the farm was to be run using traditional organic methods, so most of my memories of those first two years were of constantly pulling out weeds and carting manure around the place.

After three years, it was as if the lights came on, and everything just fell into balance. Somehow we had managed to tread water and life settled into a rhythm. That's the special thing about organic farming: Mother Nature astounds you with her abilities. At first we had to really plan carefully to ensure that all the inputs to our farming were organic, making compost and introducing animals and their fertilisers to the cycle. Now it has become second nature to eat and plant seasonally.

As I plant, fertilise or prune, I dream of how wonderful our produce is going to taste in this dish or that. The pleasure of plucking the first warm peach from a tree in a sunny orchard, and of yearning for the first tomatoes, is what food is all about for me. The smile on my son's face as he shovels a huge slice of strawberry tart into his mouth is the reward, and my happiest times have been spent eating around the old oak table on the patio of the farmhouse. Those dreams of long, lazy meals changed a bit, but were never completely abandoned after all.

The truth is that I have had to change the way I cook to adapt to our lifestyle. There's no convenience store just around the corner, and if there was, my boys would probably turn their noses up at what's in them. I've had to learn how to put quick, healthy, filling meals for kids on the table in minutes. However, I have been determined, in developing this style of cooking, to make use of what's in the garden, what comes from the animals and what we sometimes trade with neighbours or other farming friends.

It is impossible to find organic substitutes for all our needs. Flour and other staples are often difficult to find in quantity, but people are starting to demand more from their produce and the recent boom in farmer's markets has meant that there is far more access, even for city-dwellers, to good, wholesome produce. My recipes, the short-order ones and the slower dishes, are therefore designed with organic and seasonal principles in mind, but my practical nature also allows me to incorporate the best of conventional produce where I find that organic is not available.

The rewards of our lifestyle are visible in the excellent health and permanent good cheer of my family. To bring up children in a farming environment has been a true privilege. They love to help around the farm. Nic's a dab hand at rounding up the cattle on his scrambler, and Sam is very proficient at topping up barrels and cleaning out tanks. Both boys help their dad with the harvest, driving tractors and stacking crates, both completely invested in the health and productivity of their environment. As we wander around the farm together on our traditional Sunday afternoon stroll, ideas abound. We think of more trees to be planted, orchards developed, new grape cultivars to put in, and what about a herd of milking goats?

Crunch

For me the very first principle of growing things organically is to make sure we enjoy them in their natural state, or as close to it as possible. Everyone seems to be cooking with organic ingredients these days, which is wonderful, but I think we still forget what it's like to just pick something off the bush or vine, or dig it out of the soil, give it a quick wash and pop it in our mouths.

It's amazing how flavourful things actually are, when you remove the pesticides, fertilisers and other interventions used to deliver long–life, homogenous, out-of-season produce to supermarkets – food looks and tastes different. There are other advantages to growing things outside the kitchen door too, like the absence of packaging and the sheer satisfaction.

I have grown salad crops and herbs all my life, even when living in a flat on the King's Road in London. In summer I would have window boxes bursting with ingredients to add to the then popular prawn cocktails and avocado ritz salads.

One of life's great joys for me is strolling around my garden with my basket, picking and snipping at whatever's ripe and ready. There's something leafy and crunchy for our lunch and dinner table every day during spring and summer, and even autumn. Often, I just let the ingredients inspire me. There really is nothing to compare with the feeling of eating produce or ingredients you've grown yourself, especially in a salad of some kind where you can experience every flavour.

Spring Bean Salad

250g	French beans
250g	peas
250g	broad beans
200g	feta cheese
3 tblsp	good quality olive oil
handful	flat-leaf parsley

serves 6

For me this salad represents spring. Beans and peas are the first of the spring vegetables ready to harvest in the garden, and we tend to get armloads of them. Top and tail the French beans and shell the peas and broad beans. If you use very young broad beans, then you don't have to blanch them to remove the skin on the fruit. Place French beans in boiling water for 3 to 5 minutes depending on size. Do the same with the peas and broad beans, but only for 2 minutes. Remove the beans and peas and plunge into iced water to stop the cooking process. Mix beans and peas together in a bowl, add chopped feta and roughly chopped parsley, season to taste and drizzle with the olive oil.

Rocket, Fig & Goat's Cheese Salad

100g	rocket
6	ripe figs
1	ripe goat's cheese
4 tblsp	olive oil

serves 6

Rocket is one of the easiest things you could ever imagine growing. In fact, in the right conditions, it's such an aggressive and successful plant that you have to be careful where you put it because it will take over like a weed.

The price of it in a supermarket always astounds me as it really requires very little input to get bumper harvests from it. This is one of my favourite salads because it combines the sharpness of the rocket with my absolute favourite fruit.

Toss the rocket into a bowl. Quarter the figs and chop up the goat's cheese and add them to the rocket. Toss together lightly and dress with a good quality olive oil.

Salsa Verde

50g	rocket
handful	pea shoots (if available)
1	medium fennel bulb finely diced
handful	chives
handful	basil
handful	flat leaf parsley
	vinaigrette

serves 6

This recipe really is about the glory of keeping a kitchen garden. You basically just pick some green things that you think will taste nice together, put them in a bowl and eat them. What could be simpler or healthier?

Place the rocket and pea shoots in a bowl. Finely dice the fennel, chop the chives and shred the basil and parsley by hand. Add all this to the rocket and pea shoots and toss with a vinaigrette.

French Beans with Eggs

400g	French beans
2	hard-boiled eggs
4	medium spring onions
	vinaigrette

serves 6

Top and tail beans and place in a pan of boiling water for 3 to 5 minutes, depending on their size. Drain and refresh in iced water to stop the cooking process.

Finely chop the eggs and spring onions, arrange the beans on a plate and sprinkle the egg and onion over the top. Season to taste and dress with vinaigrette.

Note: I do not use salted water for any beans, as it tends to make them tough.

Tomato & Cucumber

2	large cucumbers
12	cherry tomatoes
handful	parsley, chopped
handful	mint, chopped
	zest and juice of a lemon
50ml	olive oil
	salt and pepper to season

serves 6

For some reason, all the cucumbers I grow tend to ripen at the same time,
so I make this to use them up.
Peel and seed the cucumbers, then slice and arrange them on a plate.
Halve the tomatoes and scatter them over the cucumber. Sprinkle with parsley
and mint, and drizzle with oil, season to taste, but be generous with the salt.
Leave for an hour before serving at room temperature.

Cos & Grape Salad

4	little gem Cos (or butter) lettuce
30g	white grapes
100g	toasted almonds
2 tblsp	chopped chives
	vinaigrette

serves 6

I love the idea of mixing seasonal fruits with salads; you could also use pears or apples,
but when the hanepoot grapes ripen on the farm, I always use them in salads.
Arrange the lettuce leaves on a plate. Halve and seed the grapes then scatter them
on the leaves. Add the almonds and chives, season to taste, and dress with vinaigrette.

Broccoli Salad

1	head of broccoli
6	slices streaky bacon
100g	raisins
1 tblsp	sesame seeds
150ml	honey mustard mayonnaise

serves 6 Separate the broccoli into small florettes, then slice the bacon into lardons and fry until crispy. Place all the ingredients in a salad bowl and pour over the dressing. Toss well; this salad absorbs a lot of dressing.

Variation You can really play around with this recipe. Bacon is essential and so is something sweet. I have replaced the raisins with other dried fruit and also added nuts. If you want a more filling dish, add 250g cooked penne and it becomes a pasta salad.

Courgette Salad

800g	courgette
2 tblsp	olive oil
	vinaigrette
4 tblsp	chopped fresh mint

serves 6 Slice courgettes lengthways into ribbons and then toss the ribbons in the oil. Heat a griddle pan until smoking and then cook batches of courgette ribbons to leave brown griddle marks on each side. It's very quick, about a minute per side. Place the cooked courgette in a shallow dish, and pour some vinaigrette over each batch while still hot, so the flavour is absorbed into the courgette. Sprinkle with mint and serve warm.

Orange, Rocket & Pomegranate Salad

100g	rocket
2	medium oranges
1	pomegranate
handful	toasted pumpkin seeds
	vinaigrette

serves 6

This is very much a salad of season. We grow our own satsuma oranges and they are ripe for harvest at the same time as the pomegranates in the top paddock. You could use any orange, but I love the sweetness of the satsumas mixed with the sharpness of the pomegranate seeds. It's great for entertaining too, as the colours are fantastic on a plate.

Arrange the rocket on a platter. Peel and finely slice the orange, removing any pith, and arrange on the rocket. Cut the pomegranate in half and scoop the seeds over the salad, allowing the juice to run out as well. Sprinkle the pumpkin seeds over everything, dress with vinaigrette and toss before serving.

Winter Slaw

½	white cabbage
2	fennel bulbs
2	large carrots
2	sticks celery
2	oranges
150ml	olive oil
1 tblsp	Dijon mustard
	salt to season

serves 6

Sometimes in the middle of winter, I crave something crisp and fresh after all that rich comfort food. You'd think something fresh and crunchy would be hard to come by in an apparently barren season, but with a little inspiration, you can get delicious raw food out of a winter garden.

Finely slice the cabbage and fennel. Peel and grate the carrots, trim the celery and finely slice that too. (All this slicing needs to be pretty fine, so you need a really sharp knife.) Segment one of the oranges and mix it with the fennel, carrot, cabbage and celery in a large bowl. Pour the oil into a jar, add the juice from the second orange and the Dijon mustard, shake well and pour over the salad. Season with a generous pinch of salt.

Winter Salad

½	baby butternut
	red wine vinaigrette dressing
200g	cherry tomatoes
2	garlic cloves
	drizzle olive oil
1	beetroot
½	baby cabbage sliced wafer thin
100g	rocket

Cut the butternut into fine matchsticks, place in a bowl with 100ml vinaigrette and leave for an hour. Roast the tomatoes and garlic with a drizzle of olive oil in a pre-heated oven at 180°C for 10 to 15 minutes until soft, then allow to cool. Peel the beetroot and shave it into slivers using the potato peeler. Finely shred or grate the cabbage and place it, with the beetroot and rocket, in a large salad bowl. Add the butternut with the vinaigrette in which it has been marinating and top with the roasted tomatoes. Don't toss, and serve at room temperature.

Apple & Fennel Salad

100g	rocket
2	apples
2	medium fennel bulbs
handful	pecan nuts
	honey mustard dressing

serves 6   Finely slice the fennel and apple and place all the ingredients in a salad bowl. Dress with the honey mustard dressing and serve.

Egg & Bacon Salad

8	rashers streaky bacon
6	eggs
4	little gem lettuce
2 tblsp	chopped chives
	honey mustard dressing

serves 6

This is quite an odd thing to call a salad, yet it is something we eat all the time on the farm. It is particularly scrumptious because we have fresh, organic eggs every day. When it's really hot in the valley in summer, big meals are the last thing on our minds, and an egg and bacon salad fills the gap perfectly.

Chop up the bacon and fry until crispy. Poach the eggs in a large pot of boiling water until soft, they shouldn't take more than a minute or so. If you hate poaching eggs, you can also do this with coddled eggs in one of those special pans. Place some leaves on each plate and top with an egg and some bacon. Add the chives and dress with honey mustard dressing if you fancy. I often just eat it as it comes with salt and pepper.

Tomato Salsa

600g	cherry tomatoes
1	small onion
2 tblsp	chopped oregano
	vinaigrette

serves 6

Halve the tomatoes and place in a bowl, with the finely chopped onion and oregano. Season and toss in the vinaigrette, and leave for at least an hour before serving for the flavours to blend.

Roast Tomato Bruschetta

1	baguette
8	garlic cloves for the bruschetta
500g	cherry tomatoes
bunch	fresh basil
	olive oil

serves 6

I have an old frying pan I keep specially for cooking on the charcoal fire. It's great for the odd extras you need with a braai. Pop the pan on a cooler part of the braai and toss in the whole tomatoes, roughly cut in two of the garlic cloves and add 2 tblsp olive oil. While the tomatoes are cooking, slice your baguette on the angle and place on the grill. Watch them carefully; they won't take long, and burn easily. Rub each hot slice with a garlic clove and drizzle on some oil. Then place a spoon of the hot tomatoes on top, and lastly, shred some basil onto the slices. Eat while warm.

Tomatoes

I have a tomato obsessive disorder. For me they are the ultimate food plant because you invariably get a good crop, and their culinary uses are endless – you always need tomatoes. Probably the best thing about them is that you can grow them anywhere – even on a sunny windowsill in a flat.

Over the years, I have collected an array of different seed varieties. There's a big fuss these days over 'heirloom' tomatoes, older varieties that you never come across in shops. I'm sure there are some rare varieties in my garden, but I just tend to grow ones that taste delicious and look good – red, yellow, orange, large and small, even striped ones.

My favourites are the large beefy tomatoes that are so full of flavour. I grow two varieties, Beefsteak and Marmande. One plant could give you a couple of kilos, so it's well worth planting one in a pot outside the kitchen door. Cherry tomato plants produce a particularly rewarding crop, and will keep giving you tomatoes throughout the summer.

The kitchen bursts with them at the end of summer, as they are shovelled onto trays to be roasted in the oven with garlic and herbs, and then frozen for winter sauces, stews and soups. I also plant basil with them to enjoy healthy tomatoes and basil each summer.

Nourish

Our valley sees the best of all seasons, hot summers and cold winters, and our eating and growing habits reflect these cycles. As the season turns a little colder, we tend to eat more in the way of cooked vegetable dishes. Soups are a great one, and in winter I serve soup probably too often. I love a bowl of hot soup for lunch, and so do the boys. It's the ultimate comfort food on a cold, rainy day.

The boys are fans of vegetables because they participate in the 'hunt' for their supper. Sam loves carrots and we often have a surplus in the kitchen because he's always digging around looking for the biggest carrot in the world. There's something incredibly satisfying in unearthing your own potatoes or sending the kids out to gather the makings of dinner from the garden. Preparing them is also part of the natural cycle on the farm. The peels and off-cuts go to the pigs or the compost heap to be turned into even more wonderful organic produce of one kind or another.

Of course, cooking vegetables isn't just for winter, and there are some favourites in this section that make it to the table on a weekly basis. Even when you cook organic veggies, there's something about their flavour that just sets them apart from conventionally grown produce. You don't have to have a garden to enjoy organic vegetables, as the growth in farmer's markets and box delivery schemes puts them in everyone's reach. The excess from our kitchen garden goes to an organic box delivery scheme in Cape Town each week.

Broad Bean
& Bacon Risotto

6	slices streaky bacon
2 tblsp	olive oil
6	spring onions
250g	risotto rice
1 litre	chicken or vegetable stock
250g	shelled broad beans
30g	unsalted butter
100g	parmesan cheese (finely grated)
handful	parsley

serves 6

Over a moderate heat, cook the chopped bacon with the oil in a frying pan until soft but cooked through. Add the finely chopped spring onions to the pan and cook for a few seconds before adding the rice. You need to make sure it gets well coated in oil before adding a ladle of stock. Stir continuously, and as the stock becomes absorbed, keep adding a ladle at a time. This is not a speedy process, but essential for a creamy risotto. After about 15 minutes a good two-thirds of the stock should have been added. While this is going on, bring a pot of water to the boil. Add the beans to the water (don't salt the water, it makes the beans tough) and blanch for three minutes, then strain. Add this to the risotto and keep ladling the stock. Within 5 minutes it should all be used up. Add the finely grated parmesan and the butter, remove from the heat and stir. Finally, stir in the chopped parsley and serve straight away. Risottos do not take kindly to waiting.

Roasted Roots

1kg	root vegetables
1	head of garlic
60ml	olive oil
1	bouquet garni
	salt and pepper

serves 6

You need a mix of root vegetables for this dish: parsnip, carrots, celeriac and onions work well together, but you can use beetroot and turnips too. Peel the vegetables if you want to, and chop the larger ones. Carrots and parsnips look best left whole, or halved lengthways. Others need to be chopped to similar thickness for even cooking. Place in a baking tray with the garlic cut in half across the middle. Add the bouquet garni and pour the oil over everything. Bake in a pre-heated oven at 200°C or gas mark 6 for 30 to 40 minutes, and check after 30. Remove the bouquet garni, break up the garlic, sprinkle generously and serve.

Baked Stuffed Potatoes

6	large potatoes
120g	grated strong cheddar per person
2 tblsp	butter
2 tblsp	chopped chives

serves 6

Bake the potatoes in a pre-heated oven at 180°C or gas mark 4 until soft. Slice the cooked potatoes in half lengthways and scoop out the centres. Place the hot potato from the centre into a bowl and add the cheese, butter and chives. (You may want to add some crispy bacon.) Season to taste, then mash and return to the potato 'shells'. Place under a hot grill for 5 minutes until browning on top.

Cous Cous with Tomato & Olives

250g	cous cous
250ml	warm water
100ml	olive oil
	zest and juice of one lemon
12	cherry tomatoes
100g	pitted black olives
1	medium red onion
1	handful fresh oregano
1	handful fresh parsley
	salt and pepper

serves 6

We love eating cous cous with lamb chops, and this dish really works for me at busy times on the farm. It can be made ahead and heated or quickly assembled and left to soak while I do other things. I tend to serve it at room temperature, but you can heat it, covered, in the oven before serving.

Soak the cous cous in the warm water in the bowl you intend serving the finished dish in. Leave for at least 30 minutes or up to an hour.

Chop the red onion very finely, slice the tomatoes into quarters and chop the olives and herbs. Add the zest and juice of the lemon with the olive oil to the cous cous and then stir in the rest of the ingredients and season to taste.

Sage Mash

1kg	potatoes
100ml	hot milk
100g	butter
1 tblsp	salt
handful	favourite chopped herb

serves 6

This may seem a very simple thing to write a recipe for, but when you have
really delicious potatoes, you want to do something wonderful with them.
We often simply bake them, but my boys just love mash.
Boil the potatoes in a saucepan of salted water until soft. Drain and return
to the pan, then add the hot milk and butter. Mash well, or for a very smooth
mash, put it through a moulie. Stir in the herbs and salt before serving.
(The amount of butter and milk could vary slightly depending
on the variety of potato you use.)

Potato Cakes

	sage mash (as above)
2	egg yolks beaten
50g	flour
100ml	olive oil

serves 6

Make the mash into patties using your hands. Dip into the flour (it's easiest on
a plate), then into the beaten egg and the flour again. Place in the hot oiled
frying pan and cook on each side until brown. You can keep these warm on
a baking tray in the oven if you are making a couple of batches.

Butternut, Bacon & Sage Soup

1	large butternut
1	large onion
50ml	olive oil
6	slices streaky bacon
1 litre	vegetable or chicken stock
handful	chopped sage
	crème fraiche to serve
	salt and pepper

Butternuts store very well. I always grow a large crop and store them on trays in our vegetable store for use in the winter months.

Chop up the butternut into chunks and finely chop the onion. Place on a baking tray, splash over the olive oil, add the salt and pepper and roast until tender in a medium oven. This will take about 20 minutes at 180°C or gas mark 4.

In a frying pan, lightly fry the chopped bacon. When the butternut and bacon are cool, place in a blender with your stock and blitz. Pour into a saucepan, add the sage and re-heat. Serve with a dollop of crème fraiche and warm crusty bread.

Onion Soup

8	large onions
3	cloves garlic
50g	butter
50ml	olive oil
	bouquet garni
2 litres	chicken or vegetable stock

serves 6

Onions are another crop I grow tons of, harvesting as many as 500 each January. They are dried in the sun for a couple of days and put on trays in our vegetable store. This will last till the next crop, so I have a year's supply of onions.

Peel and finely slice the onions and garlic, place in a large frying pan, with the oil and butter, and cook on a gentle heat for at least 30 minutes till the onions are soft, stirring every now and then to prevent any sticking or burning.

Transfer to a large saucepan, add the bouquet garni and stock. Cook for an hour on the same gentle heat. Remove the bouquet garni, season to taste and serve. The soup will keep in the fridge for 2 or 3 days.

Roast Tomato Soup with Gremolata

2kg	ripe tomatoes
4	cloves garlic
100ml	olive oil
1 bunch	fresh thyme
	salt and pepper
	For the Gremolata:
	zest of one Lemon
100ml	olive oil
2	cloves garlic
bunch	parsley

serves 6   A rustic, flesh-flavoured tomato soup, this will freeze well, so it's ideal for a summer tomato glut. Place the tomatoes in a baking tray and pour the oil over them. Chop the garlic and scatter it among the tomatoes. Run your fingers down the thyme twigs to remove the leaves and then sprinkle the leaves over the tomatoes. Place in a pre-heated oven at 180°C or gas mark 4 for 15 minutes. Remove from the oven and cool. There will be a lot of juice in the tray; make sure it all goes in when you transfer the tomatoes to a blender. Blitz well, but do not let it get too smooth as you want a bit of chunkiness to the soup. Pour into a saucepan and re-heat. For the gremolata, very finely chop the parsley and grate the garlic and lemon zest, add to the parsley and pour in the olive oil. Pour the soup into bowls, place 1 tsp of the gremolata on top and serve.

Farm Vegetable Soup

1	butternut
2	large onions
2	cloves garlic
2	carrots
2	mealies
200g	fresh tomatoes
200g	peas or french beans
200g	penne pasta
2 litre	chicken or veg stock
50ml	olive oil
	streaky bacon
	bouquet garni
	salt and pepper to taste

serves 6

This is the soup I make the most. It's a meal in itself, and in mid-winter it's the food Sam always asks for. This tastes so much nicer the day after it's made, when the flavours have had time to infuse, so make it ahead.

Peel and chop all the ingredients. Place the oil and chopped streaky bacon into a large pot, lightly fry the bacon. Add all your chopped vegetables and stir while they start to cook. After 5 minutes add the stock and the bouquet garni, cover the pan and cook for 2 hours on a very low heat. At this stage I leave the soup overnight. Half an hour before you want to serve, add the pasta and re-heat, season to taste and serve with warm crusty bread.

Spinach & Ricotta Cannelloni

1 box	cannelloni pasta (3 per person)
500g	spinach
250g	ricotta cheese
1	small onion
100g	strong hard grated cheese
pinch	nutmeg
	salt and pepper
	For the béchamel:
1 tblsp	butter at room temperature
2 tblsp	plain flour
350ml	warm milk
1 tblsp	Dijon mustard
100g	strong hard cheese, grated

serves 6

Over a low heat, in a small saucepan, melt the butter and stir in the flour. When amalgamated, add the mustard, take the pan off the heat, and pour in the warm milk, whisking as you pour. When the mixture has thickened (like a custard) return to a gentle heat, add the grated cheese and stir until melted. Set aside. Remove the stalks from the spinach and fry in a pan over a moderate heat for about 3 minutes, turning as it wilts. Remove from heat once the leaves have wilted and place in a large mixing bowl. Add the nutmeg and the ricotta, breaking it up with your fingers as you go. Add the grated cheese and then mix it all together with a fork. Season to taste. Fill the cannelloni with this mixture. Place the filled pasta in a greased baking dish, in two layers with a little béchamel in between. When you are done, pour over the rest of the béchamel. You can decorate it with 1 tblsp tomato sauce down the centre. Bake in a pre-heated oven at 190°C or gas mark 5 for 20 minutes or until bubbling and browning on top.

Ratatouille

8	courgette
3	medium onions
10	tomatoes (roma work well)
2	large red peppers
1	bouquet garni
4	cloves garlic
100ml	olive oil

serves 6

This is another classic dish, here is my simple version. I omit the aubergine as they don't grow well on the farm. This is heavenly with fresh bread, and I often serve it with leftover meat for a summer supper.

Peel and slice the onions. Chop the courgette into chunks, seed and chop the pepper, and cut the tomatoes into quarters, removing the seeds.

Lightly fry the onions and garlic in half the oil until soft, remove from the pan and set aside. Fry the other ingredients lightly for 5 minutes. Return the onions to the pan and add the bouquet garni. Cover the pan and cook on a gentle heat for a further 30 minutes, stirring occasionally. Remove the bouquet garni before serving. I love this cold, but it is normally served warm.

This is another dish that is infinitely better the next day.

Boulangère-style Potatoes

800g	potatoes
500ml	chicken stock
	butter for greasing baking dish
	salt and pepper
	drizzle of olive oil

Peel and slice the the potatoes thinly. Grease a baking dish and place a layer of potatoes on the bottom. Spoon over a couple of ladles of stock and season with salt and pepper. Repeat this process till you have used up all the potato slices. Drizzle over a little oil and a final pinch of salt and pepper – these need to be seasoned well, otherwise the potatoes can taste bland. Place in a pre-heated oven at 190°C or gas mark 5 and cook for an hour or until the top layer of potatoes has become brown and crispy and all the stock absorbed.

Honey-glazed Carrots

1	large bunch carrots
1 tblsp	honey
1	large sprig thyme
1 tblsp	butter

Peel the carrots. If small, leave whole, or cut larger ones to a uniform size. Boil in water until cooked but still firm. Drain the water, return the carrots to the pan, add the honey, butter and de-stalked thyme, and toss over the heat for 2 to 3 minutes until glazed. (If you prefer, you can steam the carrots first rather than boiling.)

The Kitchen Garden

The boundaries of my kitchen garden keep moving. As I grow more and more produce, I claim little pieces of farmland to plant a new crop. There's a rough plan of what goes where each season, to assist in crop rotation, but I also tend to let things take their own course. For instance, I now plant beans in rows between the vines to fix nitrogen in the soil while giving an edible cover crop.

Companion planting is also paramount for me. I have discovered and encouraged many relationships like the partnership of onions and strawberries; one is rewarded with the sweetest strawberries, and huge sweet onions. They also protect each other nicely from insects and birds.

My family battle to keep up with the ever-moving vegetable gardens. One evening I heard Sam calling that he had found the biggest carrot in the world! There he was heaving to pull a fennel bulb out of the ground. I had moved the carrots.

The tastiest fruit and vegetables you will ever eat are the ones you grow. From one small packet of seeds many meals can be made. Today, with so many different seeds available, a kitchen garden can provide endless variety to your diet. There is also the comfort to be had from knowing exactly where your food comes from and how it was grown.

Fill

Sometimes feeding Nic and Sam can seem like a full-time job. It's not that I mind cooking for them at all. But we all have totally chaotic days, when the prospect of a couple of hours in the kitchen just makes you groan. They have such active lives that they are almost permanently hungry and I have consequently developed some kitchen strategies to keep lots of wholesome things handy to turn into meals at the drop of a hat.

When they come in after school sports or from helping with the harvest or building something in the barn, there's always some food ready to hand. The obvious things are bread and cookies, which you will find in a later section, but here there are quick meals with lots of bulk for maximum energy boost.

I love making tarts and the boys love eating them. They are easy to make, and they keep well so they can be packed into lunchboxes the next day. In fact, school mates are always trying to cadge food from Nic or Sam.

There are certain things, like chicken breasts, puff pastry or pasta, roast tomato sauce or eggs, that should always be in your fridge or pantry. Some of these things are so quick and easy that the boys can make them for themselves. However, they do look forward to mother's touch, even if I'm cheating with a few things knocked together in five minutes. Filling up on quick meals isn't just for kids though, and there are a few quick dinners in this section that Mark and I enjoy together at the end of a hectic farming day with a glass of wine.

Brochettes of Lamb

1.2kg	cubed lamb (leg is best, but you could use shoulder)
24	bay leaves
2	large onions
2	red peppers
4	garlic cloves
100ml	olive oil
handful	fresh rosemary

12 skewers   You can prepare the day before, so all you have to do when you get home late and tired is toss them on the grill. Soak the skewers in cold water for 20 minutes before use to stop them burning. Cube the meat, and cut the onions and peppers into large chunks. Thread the meat, onions, peppers and bay leaves onto the soaked skewers. Chop the garlic and place into the dish in which you are going to marinade the skewers, add the chopped rosemary and oil. Add the completed brochettes and turn them in the marinade so each has been soaked. Cover the dish and leave for 24 hours. Cook the brochettes on a hot grill, turning regularly. They should take about 15 minutes, depending on the heat of your grill.
These are wonderful to cook on an outside fire as well.

Luxury Scrambled Eggs

10	eggs
150ml	single cream
100g	finely grated parmesan
handful	chives
30g	butter

serves 6 Beat the eggs, add the cream and parmesan, and place a frying pan onto a moderate heat with your piece of butter. When the butter has melted, swirl it around the pan and immediately add the egg mixture. Stir continually, for only a couple of minutes, remove from the heat before the eggs have completely set, stir in the chopped chives and serve immediately with toast or fresh bread. If you want, you can leave the chives whole and use them as garnish.

Sesame Chicken Bites

800g	chicken fillets
100g	sesame seeds
100ml	olive or cold-pressed sunflower oil
2	beaten eggs

serves 6 Cut the fillets into bite-size pieces and place in a bowl containing the two beaten eggs. Place a large frying pan over a medium heat and add half the oil as you will be cooking these in two batches. Put the sesame seeds in a bowl, and when the oil is hot, dip the egg-soaked chicken pieces into the seeds, then pop them in the pan. Cook for 8 to 10 minutes, ensuring the chicken does not burn. Drain on some kitchen towel, then serve with a salad and baguette. I always make extra as these are just as nice cold the next day for a lunchtime snack.

Broad Bean Penne

250g	broad beans, shelled
500g	penne
100g	freshly grated parmesan
handful	fresh parsley
	drizzle of olive oil
	salt and pepper
	juice of a lemon

You'll notice that I use a lot of broad beans in my cooking. They are completely delicious and very nourishing, and at one stage we were growing them commercially. They still go to the organic box delivery outfit in Cape Town every week in season. Cook the penne in a large pot of well-salted water until al dente. In a separate pan of unsalted boiling water, blanch the beans for 3 minutes, then drain. Place the pasta in your serving bowl, add the beans, stir in the lemon juice, parmesan and chopped parsley, and drizzle over some olive oil.

Roast Tomato Linguine

500g	linguine
300g	roast tomato sauce (see recipe on page 206)
50g	parmesan
	salt and pepper

Bring a large pot of well-salted water to the boil, add the linguine, and cook till al dente. In a frying pan heat up your roast tomato sauce. Pour the sauce over your pasta, grate over some fresh parmesan, add some ground black pepper. Supper is served.

Fresh Tomato Pasta

500g	cherry tomatoes, halved
500g	orecchiette or cocciolette pasta
100g	pitted, halved black olives
50g	fresh grated parmesan
500g	linguini or spaghetti
1	handful freshly chopped parsley
	drizzle olive oil
	salt and pepper

Place the pasta into a pan of well-salted boiling water and cook till al dente. Drain into a serving dish. Add the chopped olives, tomatoes and parsley, grate over the parmesan and add a drizzle of olive oil and some ground black pepper. Serve immediately.

Potato & Sausage Sauté

8	medium potatoes
600g	of your favourite sausages, cooked
50ml	olive oil
2	medium onions
	salt and pepper

Peel and chop the potatoes into large chunks, and cook in a pot of salted, boiling water, until nearly soft. Drain and set aside. Finely slice your onions and cut your cooked sausages into chunks. Heat a large frying pan over a moderate heat and add the oil. When it's hot, sauté the onions until opaque but not brown, then add the sausage and potatoes to cook for about 15 minutes. The potatoes will start to brown and the sausage will be heated through. Season with salt and pepper and serve with salsa verde salad (see recipe on page 22).

Trout Fish Cakes

2	medium trout
500ml	white wine (you can use water if you don't have wine)
1	onion sliced
½	lemon sliced
½	whole lemon
2	bay leaves
6	pepper corns
	sage mash (see recipe on page 48)
2	beaten eggs
	flour for dusting
50g	butter
50ml	olive oil

makes 6

There is an abundance of fresh-water trout in our area. Aside from serving it poached in wine with a good helping of chips, I often make fish cakes, served with a salad or roasted roots (see recipe on page 44).

Place the trout in wine or water, in a baking dish, and add the bay leaves, onion, lemon, and pepper corns. Cover with foil and bake in a pre-heated oven at 180°C or gas mark 4 for 25 to 30 minutes. When cool, take the trout from the poaching liquid, remove the skin and take the flesh off the bones. Break the flesh into a bowl of sage mash, squeeze in the remaining lemon half and mix well. Form this mix into patties. Beat your eggs in a medium bowl and fill a saucer with flour. Heat the butter and oil in a large frying pan till hot. Dip your patties into the flour, then the egg mix, then the flour again, and place into the pan. Cook for about 8 minutes per side depending on the size of the patties. They must be brown and crispy on the outside. Serve hot.

Lunchbox Pies

	puff pastry
200g	stew or any leftover meat dish
1	egg
handful	fresh herbs

This is a classic cheat that I use to fill lunchboxes and, even though it's a sneaky way of using up leftovers, the boys always ask for them. It's really simple: whenever there's a dinner the night before that leaves suitable filling, I get out some puff pastry and make pies. There are some kids at the school who have asked if they can swap their pocket money for daily lunchboxes like Nic's and Sam's.

Roll out the puff pastry and use a saucer to cut out circles of pastry. Use a tablespoon or so of filling on half of the circle, leaving about a centimetre of the outer edge clear for sealing. Sprinkle in some chopped herbs. Paint around the edge with your beaten egg, then fold the other half of the pastry over and pinch the edges together to form a kind of pasty. Repeat until all the leftovers are used up. Place on a lightly floured baking sheet and bake in a pre-heated oven at 180°C or gas mark 4 for 20 minutes.

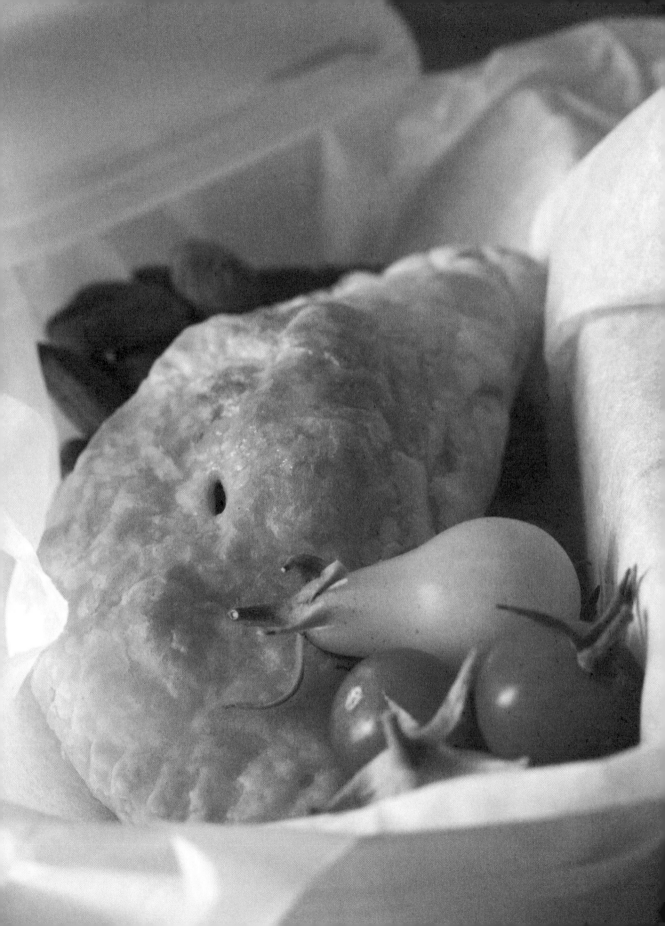

Fig & Shallot Tart

1	sheet puff pastry
8	large shallots
6	figs
50g	butter
handful	chopped fresh thyme

Roll out your puff pastry very slightly, you don't want it thin, but you need it flattened out. Finely slice the shallots and cook with the butter over a low heat until soft. Quarter the figs, add to the pan and cook for another 5 to 8 minutes. Add three-quarters of the thyme and spread the mix onto puff pastry bases cut with a scone cutter. Bake on lightly floured baking paper in a pre-heated oven at 180°C or gas mark 4 for 20 minutes. Before serving, sprinkle the remaining thyme on the tarts. Quantities are for a large metal flan case, so you will get 8 good slices or 12 little tarts.

Mushroom & Leek Tart

1	sheet puff pastry
250g	mushrooms
6	leeks trimmed and finely sliced
50g	butter
handful	freshly chopped sage
	salt and pepper to taste

In a large frying pan, cook the leeks in the butter over a moderate heat for about 15 minutes until soft. Add the sliced mushrooms to cook for a further 5 minutes. Stir in the chopped sage and pile this mix onto your tart bases. Bake on lightly floured baking paper in a pre-heated oven at 180°C or gas mark 4 for 20 minutes.

Onion & Thyme Tart

1	sheet puff pastry
4	large or 6 medium onions
1tblsp	Dijon mustard
50g	butter
handful	chopped fresh thyme
	salt and pepper to season

Fry the finely sliced onions over a low heat until soft; this will take about 20 minutes. Add the mustard, season to taste, add three-quarters of the chopped thyme and then remove from the heat to cool slightly. Pile the mixture on the tart bases and bake on lightly floured baking paper in a pre-heated oven at 180°C or gas mark 4 for 20 minutes. Before serving, sprinkle the remaining thyme over the top.

Roast Veg Tart

1	sheet puff pastry
1	large onion
1	small butternut
4	courgettes
12	cherry tomatoes
1	bouquet garni
50ml	olive oil
	pinch of salt

Chop and roast the vegetables – except the tomatoes – with a good drizzle of olive oil, some salt and a bouquet garni in a pre-heated oven at 180°C or gas mark 4 until soft. Halve the tomatoes and add them to the cooked vegetables. Spread this mix over your pastry and top with goat's cheese for a more indulgent option. Bake on lightly floured baking paper in a pre-heated oven at 180°C or gas mark 4 for 20 minutes.

Spinach & Anchovy Tart

	short crust pastry
400g	spinach (trimmed and finely sliced)
250ml	double cream
4	large eggs
10	anchovy fillets
30g	unsalted butter
pinch	ground black pepper

Made with short-crust pastry (see recipe on page 204). This is a delicious tart to make for a summer lunch: spinach and anchovies make one of the great culinary partnerships. A simple tomato salad is all you need to go with this. Again, quantities are for a large metal flan case, so you will get 8 good slices. Line your flan case with the short-crust pastry and blind bake in a pre-heated oven at 180°C or gas mark 4 for 10 minutes. I find it easiest to place a circle of baking paper on top of the pastry, and a weight on top of this. I use dried chickpeas that I keep in a jar and re-use for this purpose. While the pastry is in the oven, chop up your anchovies and place into a large frying pan with your butter, on a low heat. Stir these around till they disperse into the butter, add your fine shards of shredded spinach and stir while the leaves wilt. This will take only 2 to 3 minutes – you do not want them cooked and soggy. In a bowl, beat the eggs and add your cream, then stir in the spinach and anchovy mix, and add a pinch of pepper. You will not need to add salt because of the anchovies. Pour this mix into your pre-baked flan case and return to the oven for a further 20 to 25 minutes. Serve warm.

Tomato & Brie Tart

	short-crust pastry (see recipe on page 204)
1	dozen tomatoes
250g	camembert or brie
1 tblsp	Dijon mustard
handful	roughly torn basil leaves

This is a great dish to make if you have some old brie or camembert that's gone a little high. The quantities below are for a largish metal flan dish (28–30cm) and will give you 8 good slices. Blind bake the short-crust pastry in a pre-heated oven at 180°C or gas mark 4 for 10 minutes and set aside to cool slightly before you add the tomatoes and cheese. Brush the pastry with the mustard. Finely slice the tomatoes with a sharp knife, removing the core as you go, slice the cheese as finely as possible. Cover the flan base with overlapping slices of the cheese, tomato slices and torn-up basil leaves, until the base is covered. Return to the oven for 20 to 25 minutes, till the cheese is bubbling. Leave this flan for a good 10 to 15 minutes before serving, as the cheese will be very runny while hot. Serve with a salsa verde or simple green salad.

Potato, Cheese
& Herb Frittata

10	large eggs
1	large onion
4	medium potatoes, peeled, boiled till soft and sliced
100g	strong, hard grated cheese
30ml	olive oil
	handful of chopped fresh sage leaves
	black pepper

serves 6   A simple lunch or light supper served with a tomato or bean salad. This is also a wonderful picnic dish. Cool, then wrap in greaseproof paper and don't forget to take a knife to slice the frittata, and a chilled bottle of wine to go with it.
Fry off your onions in a large frying pan with the olive oil. When soft, add the sliced potatoes. Beat the eggs in a bowl and add the cheese, a good pinch of ground black pepper and chopped sage. Pour this mixture onto the onions and cook on a low heat – this will take 8 to 10 minutes – till firm. Place under a very hot grill for a further 2 minutes to brown on top.

Hamburgers

Makes 6 good-size patties

1kg	beef mince
2	beaten eggs
1 tblsp	mustard seeds
1 tblsp	coriander seeds
1 tblsp	fennel seeds
2	cloves garlic, grated
	salt and pepper
	drizzle of oil for cooking
1	roll per patty

In a mortar and pestle, bash up your seeds and place them in a hot frying pan for a mere minute to bring out their flavour. Put the mince into a large bowl, add the seeds, grated garlic, a good pinch of salt and ground black pepper, and the beaten eggs, and mix well. Take a handful of the mix and form a patty, then repeat till you have 6. Heat up a griddle or frying pan till it's hot. Brush a very small amount of oil onto the pan, then place the patties in it. I find they need a good 7 minutes on the one side, then 5 on the other, but this will vary slightly depending on the thickness of your patty. To test, you can push a skewer in and see if any blood comes out. I always rest mine for a further 3 to 4 minutes after I remove them from the heat. Place on a sliced roll and add whatever takes your fancy – lettuce is a must. I also like a good slice of tomato and some lightly fried onions. Serve with a good helping of homemade tomato chutney.

Lemon Chicken Breast

6   chicken breasts
50ml   olive oil
2   garlic cloves
    zest and juice of a lemon

Place the chicken breasts on a board and, with a rolling pin, give them a good bash to flatten them slightly, and then put them into a bowl. Add to this the lemon zest, 2 crushed garlic cloves and the olive oil. Marinate for an hour or thereabouts. Heat up a griddle pan, add the chicken breasts, and cook on each side for 3 to 5 minutes. When done, squeeze over the lemon juice, then remove from the pan and serve. Make this inside on a griddle or outside on the fire – simple and delicious. Serve with pasta or a salad and fresh, warm bread rolls.

Honey Soy Chicken

6   chicken breasts, cut into strips
50ml   olive oil
    zest and juice of a lemon
2 tblsp   honey
2 tblsp   soy sauce

Marinate the chicken strips in the olive oil and lemon zest for one hour. Heat up a frying pan. When hot, place the chicken strips in. These will cook quickly – about 3 minutes per side. When just cooked, add the soy sauce and honey, stir the mixture around so all the chicken is coated, and serve.

Pizza

750ml	flour
1 tsp	salt
1	sachet instant yeast
3 tblsp	olive oil
125ml	lukewarm water

This recipe is a regular treat in our house, and it will make two good-size bases. You can double the recipe and keep rolled-out bases in the freezer for quick meals in the future.

Mix the flour and salt together in a mixing bowl. Sprinkle the yeast over the top and then stir in the olive oil and water. Transfer to a floured surface and knead until well combined and the dough is smooth. Return to the bowl, cover with a damp cloth and place in a warm part of the kitchen to rise for 2 hours or until the dough doubles in volume. Divide the dough in two and roll out to the desired thickness. The thinner the base, the bigger it will be.

Toppings The base of all our pizzas is the roast tomato sauce (see recipe on page 206). You can make up your own topping. I usually use cheese, tomato, rocket and oregano, and sometimes add cooked sliced mushrooms and bacon. Bake in a hot oven 200° or gas mark 6 for 5 minutes until the cheese is browned and bubbling on top. This is a great way to get kids into the kitchen.

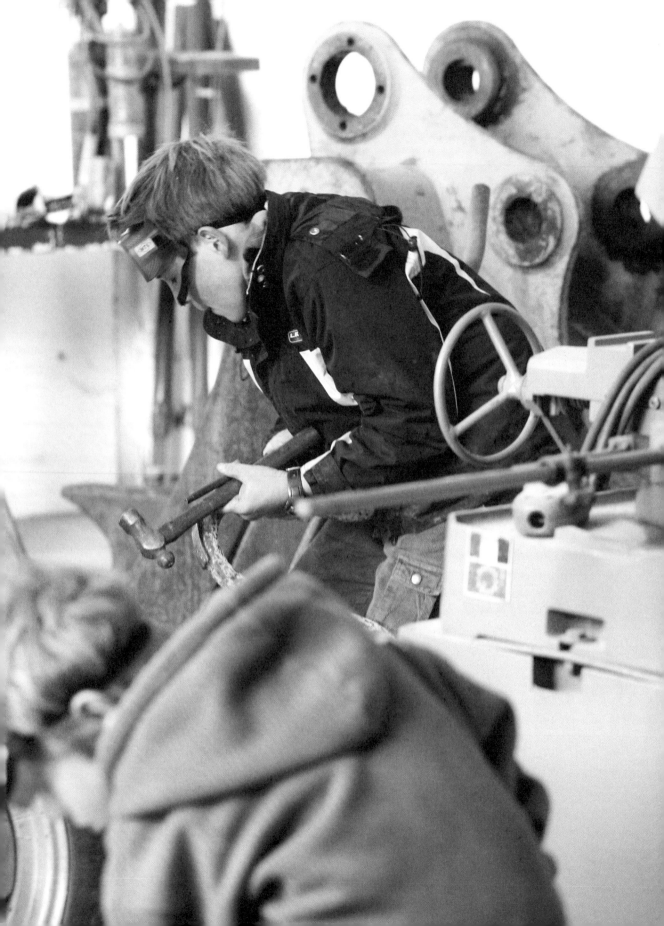

The boys

Eikenbosch farm and the life we have created is really about our boys. Mark and I enjoy a certain quality of life here, one that we both coveted for a long time, but it took Nic and Sam's arrival to focus things and get us out of the city. We wanted a place for them to breathe clean air and have active, happy childhoods.

Perhaps it worked too well. I now have that classic mother complaint that I only get to see my children when they're hungry. At least I don't have to worry about what they might be getting up to in some shopping mall. They disappear for hours on end on their motorbikes, or into the barn to build a land yacht or a boat for the river.

The pair of them are real farm boys. They seem to be able to fix or build anything, both drive tractors for us during harvest and they just love getting dirty doing odd jobs or playing around the farm. Their sense of responsibility is also incredibly well defined – Nic often takes over as de facto foreman on the farm when Mark is away on business.

All this activity takes a lot of feeding, which brings us to one of the basic reasons why we moved to the farm: a healthy lifestyle thrives on a healthy diet. An organic lifestyle provides just that, even if it does seem an endless task keeping the cookie jar full.

Comfort

My large glass cookie jar sits on a sideboard just inside the kitchen door. This is the most convenient arrangement, as it means biscuits can be grabbed by passing children and adults as they charge in or out of the house. I also find that if a few home-baked goodies are placed in a lunchbox, the temptation for them to buy sweet junk full of goodness-knows-what disappears completely.

After all, nothing really tastes as good as a homemade brownie or a chunk of cake: these are the basis of a lot of the fondest memories of my own childhood. My constant quest with this arrangement is to keep the metaphorical cookie jar full, but biscuits are quick to make so it never becomes a chore. A freshly baked cake is also not really that difficult to produce.

I bake a cake for the boys every Sunday – it's become a kind of ritual for us. For me, it's a great 'mum' thing to do, and a total joy seeing them bite into a huge slice of delight.

Another classic comfort food is bread, but the stuff we find in supermarkets barely warrants the name. Once you get into a rhythm, baking a fresh loaf every day becomes part of daily life and, of course, it makes the whole house smell wonderful. I have to admit to being a bit of a cheat in this regard, though. Years ago I was given a gift in the form of a bread machine. Never one to waste an opportunity to save time, I often use it to do the kneading for me. Believe it or not, life is very busy on the farm, so finding little time-saving tricks really helps things along.

The Famous
Stevens Brownies

Makes 24 good-sized brownies

300g	unsalted butter
300g	unrefined white sugar
4	medium eggs
100g	self-raising flour
50g	cocoa powder
50g	good quality dark chocolate

I think it was Nic who started calling these brownies 'famous', and with good reason; they are the treat most often requested by the boys and visiting friends. They are so rich and gooey that they often get used as a sweet treat for parties and as desserts for grown-ups. The joy is you can cut them to whatever size you need, although in our house it's usually 'the bigger the better.'

Blend the butter and sugar together until pale and creamy, then add the eggs one at a time. Fold in the flour and cocoa powder thoroughly before adding the chopped-up chocolate. Pour the mixture into a greased baking tin. I use one measuring 23 x 30cm – anything close to this size will work. Place in a pre-heated oven at 180°C or gas mark 4, bake for 20 to 25 minutes – the brownies should wobble slightly to retain their gooey centre when removed from the oven. Cut into squares when cool.

Lemon Polenta Cake

250g	unsalted butter
250g	unrefined white sugar
3	lemons
4	large eggs
125g	polenta
100g	self-raising flour

Cream together the butter and sugar, and add the zest and juice of two and a half lemons (save the other half for the top). Mix in the eggs and polenta and, finally, fold in the flour. Pour into a greased 20cm cake tin. Finely slice the remaining lemon half, and place slices over the top of the cake. Bake at 160°C or gas mark 3 for 30 minutes. Serve warm as a dessert or as a cake at room temperature.

Vanilla Sponge Cake

225g	self-raising flour
225g	unsalted butter
225g	unrefined white sugar
4	large eggs
½ tsp	vanilla essence

Ths is a very basic and useful cake, not dissimilar to a traditional Victoria sponge. You can bake it as a single sponge cake in a deep cake tin and pour over lemon or chocolate icing, or divide the mixture between two sandwich cake tins, fill with jam and dust with icing sugar. For a special occasion, make a sandwich cake and fill it with fresh berries and whipped cream.

Cream together butter and sugar until light and fluffy and then add the eggs and vanilla. Fold in the sifted flour and then pour into the cake tin/s you have chosen. Bake at 180°C or gas mark 5 in a pre-heated oven for 25 to 30 minutes for a single cake or 20 to 25 minute for sandwich cakes. Test by poking a skewer into the centre of the cake: it should come out clean.

Variation   For a really good chocolate cake, add 40g cocoa powder to the flour and 2 tblsp milk with the eggs.

Honey Cake

250g	clear honey
225g	unsalted butter
100g	light brown sugar
3	large eggs
300g	self-raising flour
	icing sugar for dusting

Gently heat the honey, butter and sugar in a saucepan, stirring until the
sugar has melted completely. Add the eggs to the mixture, then fold
in the flour. Pour into a cake or loaf tin lined with greased baking paper.
Bake at 180°C or gas mark 4 in a pre-heated oven for 45 to 50 minutes.
Test with a skewer to see if the cake is cooked right through.
Sieve icing sugar over the top of the cake when cool.

Almond Biscotti

Makes 12 to 14 large biscotti

175g	plain flour
175g	unrefined white sugar
50g	roughly chopped almonds (not ground almonds)
½ tsp	vanilla essence
2	large beaten eggs

Place all the ingredients into a mixing bowl and, using your hand, mix into a dough. This is a sticky job, but the mixing does not take long. As soon as the mixture comes together, place on a floured surface and, with your hands, form into a long sausage shape roughly 6cm in width and 30cm in length. Place on a floured baking tray; bake for 15 to 20 minutes at 180°C or gas mark 4 until the dough is starting to brown and is firm to the touch. Switch off the oven and remove the biscotti, closing the door immediately to conserve the heat. While the baked dough is warm, cut it into slices, laying each slice on its side on the baking tray as you go. Return the tray into the turned-off oven to dry out and crisp up. Remove when the oven has cooled down. These will keep in a tin or jar for a week.

Cheese & Herb Scones

Makes 8 to 10 scones depending on the size of your scone cutter

50g	unsalted butter
250g	plain flour
3 tsp	baking powder
100g	strong, hard grated cheese
handful	mixed thyme, parsley and oregano
150ml	milk

Cut the butter into little cubes and rub it together with the sifted flour and baking powder in a mixing bowl. Add three-quarters of the grated cheese and chopped herbs, then pour in the milk, stirring with a fork till you have a soft dough. Roll the dough on a floured board until it is about 2cm thick, then cut into rounds with a scone cutter, roll out the leftover scraps of dough and cut these out as well. Place the scones on a floured baking tray (I use a sheet of baking paper as well to prevent sticking), place the remaining cheese on each scone and bake in a pre-heated oven at 200°C or gas mark 6. You will not be able to resist eating one as you remove them from the oven, as they smell heavenly.

Cheese & Herb Bread

150ml	white wine
150ml	olive oil
4	eggs
250g	self-raising flour
100g	strong cheddar cheese
4 tblsp	mixed parsley and chives, finely chopped

This is a very interesting bread adapted from a French book I found years ago.
The thing about it is that there is no yeast in it – it relies on the wine as the rising
agent and there isn't such a long wait for it to prove. You just mix it and pop it
in the oven. I have developed lots of variations of this one, starting with different
herbs and then making sweet versions. Once you have the basic recipe, you can
pretty much do whatever you want with it.

Beat together wine and oil until frothy, then add the eggs. Fold in the flour and
cheese and, lastly, add the very finely chopped herbs. Pour into a greased loaf
tin and bake in a pre-heated oven at 180°C or gas mark 4 for 45 to 50 minutes.
This will keep for 3 to 4 days wrapped in greaseproof paper.

Date & Pecan Loaf

150ml	white wine (any will do)
150ml	olive oil
4	eggs
100g	light brown sugar
250g	self-raising flour
50g	chopped pitted dates
50g	chopped pecan nuts
5	whole pecans for decoration

This is a sweet variation of my yeast-free herb bread. It's great for tea with loads of farm butter. Beat together the wine and eggs until frothy, add the eggs and sugar, and blend. Fold in the flour, and then the chopped dates and pecans. Place the whole nuts along the top of the loaf. Pour into a greased loaf tin. Bake in a pre-heated oven at 180°C or gas mark 4 for 45 to 50 minutes.

Daily Bread

Makes 1 large loaf, 2 baguettes or 8 large rolls

10g	dried yeast (one sachet)
300ml	warm water
1 tsp	sugar
500g	strong plain flour or white bread flour
2 tsp	salt
1	egg yolk for glazing

This is my absolute standard bread dough recipe. I use it to make a basic loaf as well as hamburger rolls and my version of a seeded baguette. Start the yeast first by stirring it into the warm water and adding the sugar. In a large mixing bowl, tip the flour and salt. Make a well in the centre, pour in the yeast and water mix, and mix. I find it easiest to use one hand. When the mixture is totally blended together, tip onto a lightly floured surface and knead for 5 minutes. If you have a mixer, this can be done by using the dough hook and will only take a couple of minutes. Place the dough back into the bowl, cover with clingfilm or a damp cloth and leave in a warm part of the kitchen to rise, until the dough has doubled in size. Tip from the bowl and place in your desired greased baking tin, cover with clingfilm or a damp cloth to stop the dough from drying out. Leave for 10 to 15 minutes to rise again. Beat the egg yolk and brush over the surface of the bread before placing into a pre-heated oven at 190°C or gas mark 5. A large loaf will take approx 25 minutes, baguettes 20 and rolls 15. The bread should sound hollow when tapped and be golden brown from the glaze.

Olive Baguettes

500g	strong white flour or bread flour
250ml	warm water
50ml	olive oil
10g	dried yeast (1 sachet)
100g	olives, pitted and halved
2 tsp	salt
1	egg for glazing

Make the bread as per the white bread recipe on page 118, using water and oil instead of just water. After the first rise, place on a board and mix in the olives. I find the easiest way is by lightly rolling the dough, pouring the olives on top and then rolling up the dough into a long sausage. If you don't have a large oven, slit the dough in half and make 2 loaves. Place the sausages of dough onto a floured tray in a warm place to rise. This will take about 20 minutes. Brush the loaves with the beaten egg and place into a pre-heated oven at 190°C or gas mark 5 for about 20 minutes till golden brown on top and hollow-sounding when tapped. This bread is best eaten the same day.

Croissants

500g	plain flour or bread flour
40g	white sugar
1 tsp	salt
150ml	lukewarm water
150ml	lukewarm milk
10g	dried yeast (1 sachet)
200g	butter
1	egg
50g	melted butter

Sift the flour into a bowl and then add the sugar and salt. Combine the water and milk in a jug and add the yeast, then pour this mixture into your flour mix. Blend together by hand until you have a smooth ball, which you should cover with clingfilm and place into the fridge for 20 minutes. Place the butter between two pieces of baking paper and bash with a rolling pin until the butter makes a square of about 20cm – roll to smooth the top. Dust your surface with flour and roll your dough to double the size of your butter. Remove the paper from the butter and sandwich the butter between the dough, by placing on top of the dough and folding the dough over. Roll this out to make a long triangle roughly 60cm x 20cm. Fold a third of the dough onto itself and then fold the other fold. Repeat this by rolling and folding twice. Wrap dough in cling-film and place in the fridge for 15 minutes to rest, then repeat the rolling and folding process twice more, each time rolling and folding the dough 3 times. Place in the fridge again. I prefer to leave mine overnight so I have hot croissants in the morning with little effort, but you can leave it for as little as 30 minutes. Roll out the dough one final time to a square of about 40cm, and then cut into triangles. I find a measurement of roughly 18cm x 18cm x 12cm makes a medium-size croissant. Mix the melted butter with the beaten egg and paint each triangle with this wash. Roll each triangle into a sausage and tug in the points to form a crescent. Paint each croissant with more melted butter and egg, place on a floured baking tray and bake in a pre-heated oven at 220°C or gas mark 7 for 12 to 15 minutes until golden brown.

Shortbread

300g	plain flour
50g	rice flour (this is important as it gives the shortbread texture)
200g	unsalted butter
100g	white unrefined sugar

Cut the butter into small cubes, mix with the flour, add the sugar and work till the mixture forms a ball. Place on a greased baking tray (I use one measuring 25 x 16cm, anything roughly this size will work). Bake in a pre-heated oven at 180°C or gas mark 4 for 15 to 20 minutes till starting to brown. Cut the shortbread up while still warm, as they crisp up as they cool.

Oat Biscuits

200g	self-raising flour
200g	unsalted butter
75g	rolled oats
100g	unrefined white sugar
50g	brown sugar

Mix all the ingredients to form a stiff ball. Roll into small round balls in the palm of your hand, and place onto a floured baking tray. Press the balls down with the back of a fork; you may need to keep dipping the fork into warm water to prevent it sticking to the dough. Bake at 180°C or gas mark 4 for 10 to 12 mins till golden in colour. Place biscuits onto a baking grid to cool.

Variation   Ginger biscuits : replace the oats with 2 tblsp ground ginger.

Chocolate Hazelnut Biscuits

225g	unsalted butter
150g	unrefined white sugar
2	large eggs
300g	self-raising flour
40g	cocoa powder
½ tsp	vanilla essence
50g	chopped-up good-quality dark chocolate
50g	roughly chopped hazelnuts

Like the Famous Stevens Brownies, I get plenty of requests for these little nuggets.
They are like currency in our house and seldom last until the next day, even if I do
a double batch. This is another recipe you can experiment with by adding different
nuts and different kinds of chocolate.
Cream together butter and sugar, add the eggs one at a time, and then the vanilla.
Fold in the flour, cocoa powder, chocolate chips and chopped nuts. Place teaspoons of the
mix onto a floured baking tray, leaving spaces of 4cm between each biscuit to allow for
spreading while cooking. Bake at 180°C or gas mark 4 for 10 to 12 minutes.
Cool on a baking tray. Try not to eat all at once.

Chickens

I have kept chickens and ducks for 15 years, and would find it hard to live without them. Once you get used to eating your own eggs it's hard to eat shop-bought ones. The sheer delight of finding a few warm eggs in the morning is enough to make you want to cook or bake with them immediately.

As long as they have somewhere warm and safe to roost and they get plenty of greens and organic feed, the chickens pretty much take care of themselves. They do get moody and stop laying when it's cold and dark, but the egg supply from 20 layers is pretty steady.

Having chickens is also incredibly beneficial for the garden. They scratch and aerate the soil, control bugs, and the sweepings of straw and manure from our henhouse go into the compost heap to make incredibly good fertiliser for the vegetable garden.

My favourite breed is without doubt the Buff Orpington. They are huge with long pale golden feathers, and although they are not the best layers when they do lay, they produce delicious pale brown eggs. We also have a collection of Rhode Island Reds and White Beauties saved from a cruel battery existence. As for eating them, we rely on a farmer friend in the area for table birds. I really couldn't stand to eat one of the girls.

Feast

Although life on a working farm is far more demanding than we ever dreamed, there are those wonderful and precious times when we get to sit back and enjoy all the bounty that surrounds us. Mercifully, it isn't all quick meals between chores. Sometimes it's just a long family lunch around the table. Other times it's crowds of friends who might rock up for breakfast and only leave late that night after meals, walks, swims in the river and a snooze in the almond grove.

We love to entertain, and the fact that we make wine sort of suggests that we were always destined to host regular lunches and dinners. Having people visit us gives me the opportunity to share the bounty of the farm with people in all its diversity.

So the feast of our lives is not only about food. It has to do with the environment we live in, and the people we are lucky enough to share it with. Sometimes a fresh garden salad dressed in olive oil and a bit of sea salt is the greatest meal because of what went into growing it, and who you share it with.

We have some favourite dishes which are rich and indulgent, and easy to label as a feast. However, there are more simple things, like the harvest chicken, which are so redolent of our lifestyle that they are as much a feast of a meal as a celebration of our life. For me, the rule of thumb is to take your time, select the best ingredients and ensure you don't cook anything that keeps you in the kitchen and away from the glow around the table.

Daube of Beef

1.5kg	braising or stewing steak
2 tblsp	cooking oil
2 tblsp	flour
2	large onions, peeled and chopped
6	garlic cloves, peeled
6	carrots, peeled and chopped
1	bottle red wine
500ml	vegetable stock or water
300g	roasted tomatoes or a tin of tomatoes
1	bouquet garni
	salt and pepper

Brown the meat in the oil in a large stewing pot. You want to leave it in large chunks, as it will break up during cooking. When brown, remove it from the pot, set aside and sprinkle with the the flour. Add the onions, garlic (whole) and carrots to the pot to cook in the juice from the meat. You may need to drizzle in a little more oil, then cook for 5 to 10 minutes until the onions are soft. Return the meat to the pot, smother it with the bottle of wine, stock and tomatoes and push the bouquet garni into the liquid. Place a sheet of baking paper over the pot and add the lid. I always cook mine on top of the stove on the lowest possible setting for at least 3 hours. Season to taste. Serve with mashed potato and a baguette to mop up the juices. This is always best the day after it's cooked, when the flavours have had a chance to form a relationship.

Shin of Beef with Beans

1.5kg	shin of beef
2	large onions
1	bottle red wine
1	can of beans (I use cannellini or borlotti)
500ml	vegetable stock or water
6	garlic cloves, peeled
1	bouquet garni
	drizzle of olive oil
2 tblsp	flour
	salt and pepper to taste

Brown the meat in the oil in a large stewing pot. When brown, remove it from the pot, set aside and sprinkle with the flour. Add the onions and whole garlic cloves to the pot to cook in the juice from the meat. You may need to drizzle in a little more oil, then cook for 5 to 10 minutes until the onions are soft. Return the meat to the pot and add the bottle of wine, stock and bouquet garni. Cover with baking paper and a lid, and cook on the lowest heat for 2 hours. Add your beans and cook for a further half an hour. Season to taste and serve with roasted roots.

Sliced Beef Fillet with Herbed Butter

1.5kg	fillet
50g	herbed butter

For the marinade:

½	bottle red wine
	zest of one lemon
8	crushed garlic cloves

Mix all the marinade ingredients together, then marinate the whole fillet in this for at least an hour or overnight in the fridge. When you are ready to cook, make sure the fillet is at room temperature and slice it into portions about 1cm thick. Cook on a hot griddle or on an open fire grid for 1 minute on each side. Arrange the little steaks on a platter and place slices of herbed butter on top. Serve with a salad and bruschetta.

Burgundy-style Beef

1.5kg	chuck steak or shin of beef
225g	portabellini mushrooms
6	slices streaky bacon
12	small onions, peeled
6	cloves garlic, peeled
1	bottle red wine
500g	vegetable stock or water
	knob of butter
2 tblsp	flour
	drizzle of olive oil
	salt and pepper to taste

Brown your chunks of meat in a drizzle of oil, sprinkle with flour and set aside.
Place your chopped bacon, onions and garlic in the pan and cook for 10 minutes,
until the onions are lightly browned. Return the meat to the pan and drench with the
red wine and stock. Sink in a bouquet garni, cover with baking paper and pan lid,
and cook on the lowest heat for 2 hours. In a small pan, lightly cook the mushrooms
(left whole if small, halve the larger ones) for 3 minutes, till they start to soften and
change colour. Add them to the meat and cook for a further half an hour. Season
to taste. I like to serve this in a bowl with plain boiled potatoes or a warm baguette.
I make use of 'cheaper' cuts of meat not only to budget and use all of the animal
well, but also because they are often so full of flavour. Slow cooking helps to bring
out the flavour and tenderise the meat.

Herbed Pork Fillet

800g	pork fillets
6	bay leaves, crushed
2	cloves garlic, crushed
handful	chopped fresh sage
	zest and juice of a lemon
1	seeded and chopped chilli
	knob of butter
	salt and pepper to taste
50ml	olive oil for herb crust
50ml	oil for cooking

Pork fillet is a very under-utilised meat because people often complain that it's dry. Cooked using this poaching method, it stays nice and moist.

Roll the fillets up like sausages in a layer of foil and then a layer of clingfilm. Secure the ends by twisting. Cook in a large pan of boiling water for 20 to 25 minutes, depending on the thickness of your fillets. Remove from the foil and film. Place the lemon zest, chopped sage, bay leaves and crushed garlic and chilli onto a plate and mix with the oil. Roll the fillets in the mix until covered, then place in a frying pan with the butter and the remaining oil to sear. Turn the fillets over with tongs as each side takes on colour. This will not take more than a few minutes as the pork is already cooked through from the poaching. When completely browned, squeeze over the lemon then remove from the pan. Slice the pork on the diagonal, and serve on mashed potato with sea salt sprinkled on the top.

Roast Pork with Apples

2.5kg	loin of pork (you could also use a leg)
6	large poatoes, peeled, quartered and parboiled for 3 minutes
3	apples, quartered and cored
3	large onions, peeled and quartered
3	star anise
1	head of garlic, skin on, halved

Score the skin on the top of the pork lightly at 2cm intervals. Place in a roasting tin in a pre-heated oven at 190°C or gas mark 5 for an hour. After this time, quite a bit of fat will have accumulated in the roasting tray. Into this, toss the parboiled potato quarters, and cook for half an hour. Then add the onion quarters, apple quarters, garlic halves and star anise, return to the oven and cook for a further half an hour, checking after 20 minutes to turn the apples, onions and potatoes. Remove the pork from the tray and allow to rest for 5 minutes. While this is happening, you can return the tray to the oven to finish off the onions, apples and potatoes. Cut the pork into rustic, chunky slices and serve with the roast vegetables and fruit.

Pork Chops with Orange

6	pork loin chops
1 tsp	cumin
1 tsp	fennel seeds
2	small satsumas or clementines
50ml	olive oil
	salt and pepper to taste

Place the seeds into a dry frying pan to heat up for 2 to 3 minutes to release their flavour. Watch so they do not burn. Transfer the seeds to a bowl and add the grated orange rind and the olive oil. Marinate the chops for at least 30 minutes in this mixture. Heat up a griddle pan until smoking, place the chops on the pan and reduce the heat slightly. Cook for 8 minutes, turn the chops, add the rest of the orange, cut in halves, and cook for a further 4 to 6 minutes, depending on the thickness of the chops. The oranges will now be hot and soft; press them down with a wooden spoon to release the juices. Serve the chops with sage mash (see recipe on page 48) and honey glazed carrots (see recipe on page 60).

Gammon & Parsley Sauce

1.5 – 2kg	gammon (off the bone)

Poaching ingredients:

1	bottle white wine
750ml	water
1	onion, peeled and roughly sliced
4	garlic cloves, peeled
8 – 10	peppercorns
3	bay leaves

Parsley sauce ingredients:

2	handfuls fresh, chopped flat-leaf parsley
100ml	full-cream warm milk
2 tblsp	flour
50g	butter
300ml	of the gammon stock

This classic English dish takes me back to my childhood. It's great for a Sunday lunch, and you can use the cold leftover gammon in the week. Wash the gammon under cold running water, then place in a large saucepan with the wine, water and poaching ingredients. Bring to the boil, then simmer for 3 hours with a lid on. Remove the gammon from the pot, cover with tin foil and put on a platter to rest. Keep the gammon stock. In a small saucepan, melt the butter, remove from the heat and add the flour, stir till it has amalgamated, slowly add the warm milk and then add up to 300ml of the gammon stock, stirring continually till the mixture resembles a béchamel sauce (keep the remaining stock in the freezer for soups). Lastly, add the chopped parsley, pour the sauce into a jug and serve with the sliced gammon. I serve mash or boiled herbed potatoes with this for winter; in summer, a baguette and a green bean salad.

Farm Terrine

1kg	pork mince
8	slices streaky bacon sliced into lardons
	zest and juice of a lemon
250g	breadcrumbs
4	garlic cloves, peeled and finely chopped
handful	chopped fresh sage
handful	chopped fresh thyme
	large pinch of salt and pepper

Place all the ingredients in a large bowl and mix together thoroughly. I use my hands for this; it's easier. Line a terrine dish with a layer of heavy-duty foil, leaving enough to cover the top (if you don't have a terrine dish, use a loaf tin). Press the mixture into the dish or tin, and make sure you press it down well, so it is compacted. Cover with the remaining flap of foil and place in a deep roasting tin. Transfer to a pre-heated oven at 180°C or gas mark 4 and then fill the roasting tin with water until it reaches halfway up your terrine dish or tin. Bake for 2 hours, checking the water level after 1 hour and topping up if necessary. Remove from the oven to cool. You will now need to place a heavy weight on top of the terrine to compact it more; for this I use a clean brick, but anything heavy will do. Place in the fridge overnight. The next day, remove the weight and take the terrine from the dish or tin and unwrap it. Cut into thick slices and serve at room temperature. Any leftovers will keep for 4 to 5 days in the fridge, and they also freeze well. I always serve with chilli jelly.

Slow Roast Lamb

2kg	leg of lamb
handful	chopped fresh rosemary
handful	chopped fresh oregano
1 tsp	sea salt
	drizzle of olive oil

We started keeping a few sheep in the almond grove a few years ago and, in exchange for a very happy and well-fed life, they give us superb meat. It probably has something to do with the incredibly lush grass that grows under those old trees. Crush the garlic and mix with the herbs, rub a drizzle of oil on the lamb and then coat with the chopped herbs and garlic. Place in a roasting tray and cook for 4 hours at 160°C or gas mark 3. Leave to rest for 10 minutes before serving. I serve this with roast potatoes and carrots.

Marinated Lamb Chops

12	rib lamb chops
50ml	olive oil
3	garlic cloves, peeled and chopped
handful	chopped fresh rosemary
	zest of 1 lemon

Mix the oil, garlic and rosemary in a bowl and add the chops. Leave for 30 minutes. Heat up a griddle pan and cook the chops for 3 to 5 minutes per side, depending on how pink you like your lamb. These are great cooked on the braai.

Lamb Ragù

1kg	minced lamb or beef
1	large onion, very finely chopped
50g	streaky bacon cut into lardons
4	garlic cloves, finely chopped or grated
2	carrots, very finely chopped
2	sticks celery, very finely chopped
375ml	red wine
500g	tomatoes, blanched, peeled and finely chopped
1	bouquet garni
100ml	olive oil
	knob of butter (if using fresh tomatoes)

Place the oil in a large pan and fry off the chopped vegetables until softened; this will take about 5 minutes on a medium heat. Add your minced meat of choice, and let it take on colour, then pour over the red wine. In a separate pan, cook your chopped peeled tomatoes for 5 minutes, then add to the meat; if using tinned tomatoes they can be added immediately. Tip in the wine and immerse the bouquet garni, and let this simmer on a gentle heat for 2 to 3 hours, stirring occasionally. A correctly made ragù completely transforms a bowl of pasta, lasagne or cottage pie, but it takes time. Make in a huge batch and freeze – it will become the most useful thing in your freezer.

Pot Roast Chicken

1	large free-range chicken or 2 small
2	onions, chopped
6	carrots, peeled and chopped
6	potatoes, peeled and chopped
2	fennel bulbs, chopped (or you could use two sticks celery)
1	bouquet garni
½	bottle wine
300ml	water
50ml	olive oil
	salt and pepper top taste

This is the ultimate one-pot meal, and a regular visitor to the table come harvest time. It actually goes by the name of Harvest Chicken in our house because I can bung it in a pot and forget about it while we get the grapes in and have a delicious meal ready with very little fuss.

Brown the chicken in a large saucepan with the oil, and add the chopped vegetables, tipping them all around the chicken. Add the bouquet garni and tip in the wine and water, cover with a piece of greaseproof paper and pop on the lid, simmer on a low heat for 60 minutes, remove the lid and paper, and cook uncovered for a further 30 minutes. Season to taste and serve in large bowls. Any left-overs in the pot can be used as a soup the next day by adding some chicken stock.

Fennel Chicken

6	leg and thigh chicken pieces
1	onion
1	celery stalk
125g	streaky bacon
3	cloves garlic, crushed
1	knob butter
6	brown mushrooms
6	baby fennel bulbs
1	small lemon
250ml	white wine
250ml	chicken stock
	olive oil
	salt and pepper

Brown the chicken in a little olive oil until the skin is nice and crispy. Remove from the pan and set aside, then finely chop the onion, celery and bacon and fry these with the garlic in the juices from the chicken and the butter. Add the mushrooms when the onions are soft and season to taste, cooking for a further 5 minutes. Add the wine, the juice of the lemon and the stock and bring to the boil, then remove from the heat. Place the fennel on the base of a casserole dish, top with the chicken and then pour the onion mixture over everything. Place uncovered in a pre-heated oven at 200°C or gas mark 5 for 45 minutes to an hour.

Lemon & Herb Roast Chicken

1	large free-range chicken or two small ones
½	a head garlic for each chicken
½	lemon for each chicken
1	large sprig oregano
	sea salt
	knob of butter

I could cook this every night of the week and still have the boys clamouring for more. It's easy to forget just how good a roast chicken can be, especially if it is done with an organic, free-range bird.

Place the garlic, lemon and herbs inside the chicken, rub the skin with a knob of softened butter and sprinkle over a generous pinch of sea salt. Place into a pre-heated oven at 190°C or gas mark 5. A large chicken will take about 1½ hours, and a small one an hour. The lemon will keep the chicken moist. Let the bird rest for 10 minutes before carving. If serving roast potatoes, parboil the potatoes, then toss in a little seasoned flour and add to the chicken 40 to 45 minutes before it's due to come out of the oven. Check the potatoes and baste with the chicken fat a couple of times during the cooking process. In summer I serve this with a salad, in winter with a large bowl of vegetables.

Honeyed Duck Breasts

1	duck breast per person
1 tblsp	honey per breast
1 tblsp	white wine per breast
	sea salt

Score the fat on the duck breasts at 2cm intervals. Heat up a frying pan, and when it's really hot, place the breasts in fat side down. Let them sizzle away until they take on a wonderful brown colour; this will take about 5 minutes. A lot of fat will have seeped out of the duck: pour most of this into a bowl and set aside to use for cooking potato wedges at a later date (this fat will keep in the fridge for at least 4 weeks). Turn the beasts over and reduce the heat, and cook for another 3 to 5 minutes depending on how pink you like your duck. Turn the breasts again to crisp up the skin – this will take a minute. While they are turned, spoon your honey onto the duck, which is now skin side down. Remove from the pan, and rest for 3 minutes. Add the wine to the pan to deglaze. Slice the duck and pour over the honey sauce from the pan. Serve with sage mash (see recipe on page 48) or, better still, potatoes roasted in duck fat.

Animals

We believe it is impossible to run an organic farm without animals: they provide all our fertiliser and a huge chunk of charm. They have been the source of hilarious high jinks, with horses decimating apple crops in the middle of the night, bulls going walkabout on neighbouring farms, and geese occupying the swimming pool. Stompie, a huge Percheron, arrived first. He is all thundering hooves and incredible good nature, but the boss is Ulysses, a huge shire who presides over his domain, as his name suggests, like a Greek god.

The dairy herd started with just two cows that arrived just after we bought the farm with Thomas the little bull in tow. They have provided us with gallons of real Jersey milk, the base of so many wicked desserts. Since then, the grand old Duke of Pork has arrived and sired many little dukes, and sheep graze under the almond trees.

To be able to produce our own meat was an essential part of our farming plan. I worried that the boys would have a problem with this reality of farm life, but they've grown up with it and now Sam often rubs the pigs' rumps and wonders how much bacon we'll get from them. It is important that our animals lead a healthy, natural existence, and our children have grown up understanding – sometimes eagerly anticipating – the cycle of life.

Indulge

Before having children, I cooked desserts under duress. Apart from a few family recipes that had been handed down, quite honestly it was easier to do a cheese board and serve some fancy chocolates with coffee at a dinner party. The absolute joy that a tasty home-cooked pud gives my kids and their friends has changed all that. If I didn't produce a wonderful treat to finish off the meal at weekends, I would be traded in for another mum.

Looking in the fridge for leftover dessert on a Saturday morning is an added plus. I suspect sometimes that they deliberately leave some behind just so they can sneak to the fridge for an indulgent spoonful of last night's crumble. The boys have to be up pretty early if they want to get in ahead of Mark's sweet tooth though.

There is a lot of inspiration all around me on the farm for indulgent things. Mark keeps bees in the almond grove and they give the most delicious honey. Almonds are an obvious invitation to make sweet treats, and our fruit just begs to be used in puddings.

Having a little herd of Jersey cows also ensures a ready supply of rich milk and cream. Once you've made ice cream with Jersey milk, you'll wonder how it's even possible to use anything else. There is always ice cream in the freezer, as there is always plenty of cream and lots of fruit to flavour it with. My personal favourite is fig ice cream, but I've also managed to pass on my love for classics like baked custard and bread and butter pudding to the boys. After all, what is life without a little indulgence?

Figs Baked with Honey & Almonds

1	fresh fig per person
1 tsp	honey per person
1 tsp	chopped almonds per person
	water

I have about half a dozen fig trees on the farm, but I could happily have more as they really are one of my absolute favourite fruits. Little hands are always at the fruit while it's still on the branch, so getting a harvest in is sometimes hard, but I am certainly never at a loss for things to do with them when they are ripe. Cut a cross on the top of each fig and give it a squeeze to force it open a little. Place the figs in a shallow baking dish with about 1cm of cold water to stop them sticking and burning. Drizzle half a teaspoon of honey over each fig. Place in a pre-heated oven at 180°C or gas mark 4 for roughly 15 minutes, and then remove from the oven. The figs should be soft but holding their shape. Remove from the baking dish. Sprinkle some almonds on each fig and drizzle with the remaining honey. Leave for 5 minutes before serving, so that the honey seeps into the figs. Serve warm with a scoop of vanilla ice cream.

Baked Custard

6	large eggs
1 litre	full fat milk
½ tsp	vanilla essence
100g	unrefined white sugar
½ tsp	ground nutmeg
1 tsp	butter for greasing the bowl

Scald the milk in a pan – do not let it boil. Beat the eggs, and add the sugar and vanilla. Whisk the milk into the egg mix in a steady stream. Lightly butter 6 large shallow ramekins. Pour the custard mixture into a jug through a sieve: this will ensure a smooth custard. Now place the ramekins into a deep baking tray with enough hot water to come halfway up the sides. Pour the custard into the ramekins, distributing it evenly. Place this bain-marie in a pre-heated oven at 180°C or gas mark 4 for 25 minutes, then remove and sprinkle over the nutmeg, and return to the oven for a further 5 to 10 minutes.
The custard should be just firm and browning on top.

Fig Bread
& Butter Pudding

6	croissants (if you have old stale ones, all the better)
2	medium eggs
1	cup milk
4 tblsp	white sugar
4 tblsp	fig preserve
	knob of butter for greasing the baking dish

Slice the croissants, place half of them into the bottom of a buttered baking dish, and make sure the bottom of the dish is covered with the croissants. Spoon over the preserve and top with the remaining slices of croissant. In a jug, beat the eggs and add the milk and 3 tblsp sugar. Pour this mixture over the top of the pudding. Leave for 5 minutes for the custard mix to soak well into the croissants. Sprinkle the remaining sugar over the top of the pudding. Place into a pre-heated oven at 180°C or gas mark 4. Bake for 15 minutes until the top has turned a golden brown. I use the fig preserve to make this; you could use raspberry or strawberry jam as an alternative.

Plum & Almond Crumble

800g	plums
100g	white sugar
	zest of a lemon
	For the crumble mix:
120g	plain flour
100g	unsalted butter
100g	light brown sugar
30g	ground almonds
20g	extra butter for crust

Crumbles are absolute heaven once you realise how easy they are to make. I can't count the variations I've invented for the boys, using different combinations of fruit. They particularly like the toffee-like mess formed from the sugar and juices of whatever filling is being used, which bubbles out of the crumble while it bakes. Place whole plums into a saucepan, cover with water and cook gently, with the lid on, for 10 to15 minutes until they start to soften. Cool slightly and then peel, quarter and remove the stones. Add the lemon zest and sugar to the plums, and toss together. Place this mix in a large greased pudding dish. Place the crumble ingredients in a bowl and rub together with your fingers to form large crumbs. Top the plum mixture with this, along with 4 or 5 small knobs of butter. Bake in a pre-heated oven at 180°C or gas mark 4 for 20 to 25 minutes until golden brown on top.

Blackberry, Apple
& Lavender Crumble

400g	apples
400g	blackberries
50g	light brown sugar
2	sprigs fresh lavender

For the crumble:

120g	plain flour
100g	unsalted butter
100g	light brown sugar
20g	extra butter for crust

Blackberries are a particularly abundant crop; they grow like weeds and their fruit is a real treasure each summer. You need a bit of space with an out-of-the-way corner for them as they really run mad and get a bit unsightly when they die back. However, for all the puddings and jams you can get out of a single harvest, putting in some berries is well worth the effort.

Peel the apples and slice thinly. Arrange the slices in layers in a greased shallow baking or pie dish, then scatter the blackberries and sugar over everything. Pull the small lavender flower petals away from the stem and sprinkle into the fruit mix. Place the crumble ingredients in a bowl, and rub together with your fingers to form large crumbs. Top the plum mixture with this, along with 4 or 5 small knobs of butter. Bake in a pre-heated oven at 160°C or gas mark 3 for 40 to 45 minutes or until golden brown on top.

Orchard Tart

1	sheet puff pastry
1kg	assorted fruit
100g	sugar
	knob of butter
1	beaten egg

I make this with autumn fruits – it looks really wonderful and is so easy to make.
The choice of fruit is up to you, but the following all work well (use a selection
of three to four fruits): apples, pears, plums, nectarines and grapes.
Roll out the pastry to make a square about 40cm x 40cm, then place the peeled
and sliced fruit in the centre in a pile. Scatter the sugar over the fruit and top
with the butter. Fold the corners of the pastry back over the pile of fruit, leaving
a gap at the very centre, but making sure the sides meet. Brush the entire pie
with beaten egg, place onto a greased baking tray and bake at 190°C or gas mark 5
for 25 to 30 minutes, until the pastry is golden brown. Take the pie to the table
whole and serve with cream or ice cream.

Vanilla Ice Cream

400ml	full or single cream farm milk
100g	unrefined white sugar
120ml	water
1	vanilla pod
3	large egg yolks

We are really spoilt on the farm by having an almost constant supply of delicious, creamy Jersey milk. This allows us the luxury of things like ice cream whenever we fancy it. You will notice in the ingredients list that you can use farm milk or single cream – the full-cream milk you get in a supermarket won't do for this, so if you have to, buy single cream.

Scald the milk but do not let it boil. Remove from heat and add the split vanilla pod. In a separate pan, bring the water and sugar to a gentle boil, stirring until all the sugar dissolves completely. Leave it to boil for about 3 minutes to thicken the syrup. Trickle the hot syrup into the 3 beaten egg yolks, whisking constantly as you pour. The mixture will thicken slightly. Now whisk in the milk to form a creamy, thin custard. Set aside to cool, then pour through a sieve into your ice cream machine or into a plastic tub. If you are using the freezer method, stir every 30 to 40 minutes to stop crystals forming.

Variation   Use the vanilla base but add 2 tsp instant coffee and 2 tblsp fresh-ground coffee beans to the hot milk. You can also add 125ml chopped hazel nuts with the coffee for variety, or just use them as garnish when you serve the coffee ice cream.

Fig Ice Cream

500g	black figs
100g	unrefined white sugar
200ml	full-cream milk
	zest of 1 lemon

Apart from the benefits of a fat, happy little herd of Jerseys, one of my real kitchen indulgences was my ice cream machine. It certainly isn't a great big fancy thing with a built-in freezer; it's just a churn with a bowl that needs to go in the freezer for a bit before you use it. It seemed so extravagant at the time, but it has made hundreds of times its weight in ice cream. I experiment endlessly with flavours and recipes, and this 'custardless' fig ice cream is one of the easiest and the one we make tons of in fig season. Place the figs in a blender, blitz until creamy, then add all the other ingredients and blitz again. Pour the mixture into an ice cream machine, and switch on, checking every now and then for consistency. It should take about 30 to 40 minutes to churn. If you are using a plastic tub in the freezer, stir the mixture every 30 to 40 minutes until frozen, to stop crystals forming.

Variation   In summer replace figs with fresh berries – strawberries and raspberries work well, although you need to adjust the sugar content to compensate for the tartness of different fruits. I also sometimes make lollies by putting the mixture into individual moulds with sticks, making a great summer treat for the boys.

Saffron & Orange Rice Pudding

100g	risotto rice
1 litre	full-cream milk
50g	unrefined white sugar
	zest of 1 small orange (I use our satsumas or clementines in season)
1	pinch of saffron soaked in 1 tblsp warm water
1 tblsp	butter

Place the rice, milk and sugar in a saucepan to heat gently until half the milk is absorbed, stirring continually to prevent sticking. Do not let it boil. Stir in the orange zest, saffron and water, then pour into a buttered, shallow baking dish. Place in a pre-heated oven at 180°C or gas mark 4 for 45 to 55 minutes until the pudding has browned on top and the creamy rice cooked.

Sautéed Oranges

1	satsuma (or clementine) per person
1 tsp	honey per person
50g	chopped almonds

Peel and finely slice the satsumas, place in a frying pan on a gentle heat and cook for about 3 minutes until warmed through but keeping their shape. Pour in the honey and heat for about 3 more minutes, until it has dissolved. Sprinkle with almonds and serve with ice cream.

Lemon Tart

	short-crust pastry (see recipe on page 204)
2	large whole eggs and 2 yolks
150g	unrefined white sugar
180ml	full cream milk (Jersey if possible) or single cream
3	large lemons, zest and juice
1 tsp	butter for greasing the tin

This tart is a regular visitor to the table in autumn when my trees are groaning with lemons. Our meals are starting to get richer and this dessert cuts through the heaviness to provide a fresh, sharp flavour to finish with.

Line a greased tart tin with pastry, and set aside. Beat the eggs and yolks together, add the juice and zest of the lemons and the sugar, and then stir in the milk. Transfer the mixture to a jug, then place your tart case on its shelf in the oven and carefully pour the filling into it. Bake in the pre-heated oven at 180°C or gas mark 4 for 20 to 25 minutes. The tart should not be set hard but should have a slight wobble. Cool and serve at room temperature.

Rich Chocolate Tart

	short-crust pastry (see recipe on page 204)
3	whole eggs and 2 egg yolks
300g	good quality dark chocolate
150g	unsalted butter
50g	white unrefined sugar
1 tsp	butter for greasing the tin

This very rich and indulgent tart is best served at room temperature. You can
add berries on the side, but it does not need to be adorned with cream.
Roll the pastry, line your tart tin, and blind bake at 180°C or gas mark 4 for
10 minutes. Meanwhile, melt the chocolate in a double boiler with the butter
to form a silky sauce. In a separate bowl, whisk the eggs with the sugar until
pale and smooth. When the chocolate has melted, stir it into the whisked egg
mixture. While it's still hot, gently pour the filling into your pastry case. Do this
on the pulled-out oven shelf, if you can, to avert spilling while transferring
to the oven. The tart should cook in the oven at 180°C or gas mark 4 for a further
8 to 10 minutes. The filling should have a wobble and not be completely set.
Cool before serving.

Almond Tart

short-crust pastry (see recipe on page 204)

300g	ground almonds
300g	unsalted butter
300g	unrefined white sugar
3	medium eggs

This tart is inspired by the almonds that come in from our trees. It has become the indulgence that I make most often, and is utterly delicious served warm or cold. I often serve it with a dessert spoon of brandied cherries. Again, I use a metal tart tin with a loose base; anything around 28cm x 30cm in size will work for these quantities. Line the tin with the pastry and bake blind for 10 minutes at 180°C or gas mark 4. In a blender, blitz the sugar and butter until creamy, add the eggs one at a time, and then the ground almonds. Spoon this mixture into your pastry case and smooth the top with a spatula. Return to the oven and bake for 25 to 30 minutes. The filling should be set and the top turning a pale golden brown.

Strawberry Tart with Almond Pastry

	short-crust pastry (see recipe on page 204)
1.5kg	fresh strawberries
100g	redcurrant jelly (or apricot)
*	add 50g ground almonds with the flour when you make the pastry

Line a 28cm x 30cm loose-based tart tin with the almond pastry. (It's important to use this type of tart tin as the pastry case has to be removed from the tin to look spectacular.) Bake blind for 15 minutes in a pre-heated oven at 180°C or gas mark 4, and then turn the oven down to 160°C or gas mark 3 for the last 5 minutes or so. This should ensure your pastry case is evenly cooked to a pale golden-brown colour. Cool the case and carefully transfer it from the tin to a cake stand or the plate on which you intend to serve the tart. Hull the strawberries and, if you have different-size strawberries, cut the larger ones in half. Arrange them attractively in the pastry case. (I find starting at the outside and working around and in is easiest.) Push the strawberries close together so you don't see any pastry. Melt the jelly in a pan and pour over your tart. Leave for about an hour for the jelly to cool, and serve with whipped cream.

Almonds

At first we didn't quite know what to make of the collection of gnarled and ancient-looking trees arranged in a grove overlooking the stables. They were pretty in a battered way, and we knew they were almond trees, but at over two hundred years old, we were sure they must be past their prime. Imagine our surprise when they produced a massive crop of the sweetest almonds.

A few years back, one of the vicious winds that sometimes howl up the valley in winter knocked one of these venerable trees over. The wood was so hard it could not be cut with a saw and we had to haul it out of the grove by brute force. That huge trunk now rests outside the farm office as a rugged natural sculpture. Other than that, the trees have become a focal point on the farm, surrounded by lush grass which feeds our four sheep. In spring and summer we often picnic in the grove with guests, because that spot offers a perfect view over the rest of the farm.

In July they are capped with a pale pink haze of blossoms, a welcome relief from the grey winter days. Mark took one look at those delicate flowers and moved most of his beehives into the grove. The bees have a lot of flowers to choose from all over the farm, so we don't get single-blossom honey, but it's nice to know that these beautiful trees add their sweetness to another farm product.

Hoard

All the outside activities move inside each autumn, straight after our grape harvest. As the vine leaves start to turn red and gold, so begins the winter hoarding. Butternuts, onions and garlic are dried and put onto racks in our vegetable storeroom so that the air can circulate around them to prevent any rot or mould setting in. Tomatoes are dried either in the direct sun or in my drying machine, and tray-loads are roasted to store in the freezer and to be bottled for ketchup.

Whatever variety of fruit is ripe at this time is turned into jams and jellies or preserved in syrup for the winter ahead. The windfall apples in particular are gathered to form the base of herb and chilli jellies. These keep us going through the cold winter days and make wonderful gifts. The almonds are dried on the storeroom roof and then stored in baskets, while the last of the hanepoot grapes are dried on a sheet for raisins. The last crop to gather is always the olives: these I brine in a traditional method which was taught to me by a farming friend in Provence.

There is so much activity and so many things that are done at this time of the year that it is hard to do justice to them here; they are probably the topic of an entire book. In this section I have provided some recipes which I use every year and which are the building blocks for various kinds of preserved produce. It is also a section of basics to provide the dressings, pastries and stocks which I use so often in the recipes in the rest of this book.

Curing & Bottling Olives

When harvesting olives, carefully separate black from green and discard any over-ripe ones. Wash to remove any grit, then place in 20 litre buckets up to two-thirds full. Fill to the top with water and then add 250ml coarse sea salt for every 4 litres of water. For black olives, change the brine each day for 15 days; for green olives, daily for 10 days. After this, change brine weekly for 4 weeks when the green olives should be ready to bottle. Black olives take up to 6 months, changing the brine monthly. If a scum appears just scoop it off and change the water. Mix 50% water and 50% white wine vinegar, place in a large pot and bring to the boil. For each litre of this mixture add 1 tblsp salt, 3 bay leaves, 8 pepper corns, 3 small rosemary sprigs and 2 pieces of orange peel, peeled with a potato peeler. Take off the heat and cool. Fill sterile jars with olives and pour over the mixture, leaving a gap of about 1cm at the top. Drizzle some olive oil on top so you have a thin film of oil covering the brine, and then seal the jars. They will be ready to eat in 4 weeks and keep for up to a year.

Tapenade

300g	pitted green or black olives
2 tblsp	capers
6	anchovies
½	seeded chilli
	juice and zest of half a lemon
2	garlic cloves
1 tblsp	chopped thyme
100ml	olive oil

Place all the ingredients except the olive oil in a blender or a mortar and pestle and process or pound until you have a rough chunky mix. Slowly drizzle in the oil and mix. This will keep in the fridge for 2 weeks in a sealed jar.

Fig Preserve

Make this at the end of summer, and bottle and save it for those cold rainy days of winter. To serve with cheese, it is runnier and chunkier than a jam. Do use the thyme: it goes so well with figs and adds to the depth of flavour.

Cut figs in half lengthwise, combine with the water, add the sprig of thyme, bring to the boil and then simmer for about 10 minutes. You want the figs soft but not falling to pieces. Add lemon juice, zest and sugar, boil rapidly for a further 10 to 15 minutes until the juice starts to thicken. Remove the thyme, and spoon into hot, sterilised jars. Leave to cool. This will keep for 3 months sealed. After opening, store in the fridge.

Cherries in Brandy

Cherries are my favourite fruit; we are lucky on the farm as it's cold enough in winter to grow them, and it's a joy to see a laden cherry tree. They always make me feel Christmassy, as they drip with red jewels, and cherry harvest in the Cape takes place in December. When I have had my fill of cherries we always preserve some in brandy, to keep for winter. Sterilise the storage jars you intend to use and pack them with cherries – you can leave the stalk on if you wish. I use a mix of 350g white sugar to 1 litre of brandy. Dissolve the sugar in the brandy, and pour over the cherries. Seal and keep in a cool dark place; they will be ready after 3 months.

Orange & Rosemary Marmalade

Makes 6 to 7 medium jars

1kg	oranges
2	lemons (unwaxed)
2kg	granulated sugar
3 litres	water
3 tblsp	finely chopped fresh rosemary

I love the combination of orange and rosemary; it adds a wonderful, faint herby depth to a basic marmalade. Traditionally, this should be made with a bitter Seville orange, but I make mine with our early clementines which are also a little bitter. Buy early season oranges: they will not be as sweet as the later ones.

Peel the oranges and lemons and cut chunks of about 1cm². Slice three-quarters of the peel into fine slices and discard the remaining peel. Place the peel and fruit into a large bowl, cover with the water and soak overnight. Next day, transfer the fruit and water to a large pot and bring to the boil, then simmer for 40 to 45 minutes to soften the peel. Heat the sugar in a baking dish in a medium oven for 5 minutes, then add to the fruit and water. Turn up the heat and let the mixture boil for about half an hour. Remove any scum that floats to the top with a tablespoon, and stir the mixture occasionally to check for sticking. The marmalade should now have thickened quite a lot. Do the saucer test to check. Place a teaspoon of the mixture onto a saucer, put it in the fridge for 5 minutes, and with your finger test the thickness of the mixture. If you feel it's not set enough, boil a little longer. Remove from the heat, stir in the rosemary, ladle into sterilised jars, and then seal. Marmalade will keep for a year in a cool dark place.

Rich Short-crust Pastry

Enough for one large tart

250g	plain flour
175g	unsalted butter
1	egg

Rub the flour and butter together, until the mixture resembles breadcrumbs. If using a processor, be careful not to overmix. Beat the egg and then add to the mixture. Mix till it forms a ball, and let the pastry rest for 20 minutes before rolling out.

Easy Puff Pastry

Makes 500g of pastry

250g	plain flour
250g	unsalted butter in small cubes
100ml	iced water
	pinch salt

Place the flour in a large bowl, add the butter and salt, then rub together with your fingers – you don't want a smooth crumb, and the cubes should be slightly squashed up into the flour. Pour in the iced water while you mix with your other hand until all the water is absorbed. Knead the dough with your hands for a minute; there should still be some small pieces of butter visible in the dough. Cover and place in the fridge for 20 minutes to rest. Lightly flour your work surface and roll the dough into a rectangle of about 15cm x 10 cm. Fold the dough into three. Turn the dough 90° and repeat the rolling and folding. Wrap the pastry in clingfilm and rest in the fridge again for 20 minutes. Repeat the rolling, turning and folding process again, rest in the fridge and repeat for a third time. Now the pastry is ready, rest again for 20 minutes. The pastry will keep in the fridge for 2 days well wrapped in clingfilm.

Vegetable Stock

½ kg	mixed vegetables (carrots, celery, onions, leeks, parsnips and turnips)
2 litres	water (or half water, half white wine)
1	bouquet garni

Having a good stock on standby means you can quickly rustle up a delicious soup or casserole at short notice. Chop everything into large chunks and place it in a large pot with the liquid and herbs. Bring to the boil, then turn down the heat and simmer for 2 to 3 hours. Strain and use or freeze.

Chicken Stock

1kg	chicken bits (I often use wings)
1	onion
1	large carrot
1	bouquet garni
1 litre	water (or half water, half white wine)

Place the chicken and peeled, chopped vegetables in a baking tray and place in a hot oven for about 10 minutes until the chicken has taken on some colour. Transfer everything to a large pot, and add the bouquet garni and liquid. Bring to a boil, then simmer for an hour. Strain off the liquid and store or freeze until required.

Roast Tomato Sauce

2kg	tomatoes
4	garlic cloves, crushed
3 tblsp	thyme leaves
2 tsp	sea salt
50ml	olive oil

Halve or quarter the tomatoes and spread them in a baking dish. Sprinkle with all the other ingredients and roast in a pre-heated oven at 200°C or gas mark 5 for 20 minutes. Cool before whizzing in a blender. Freeze in individual portions.

Tomato Chutney

3kg	fresh tomatoes
4	onions
150ml	cider vinegar
100g	light brown sugar
2	peeled cloves of garlic
½ tsp	mustard seeds
1 tsp	allspice
1 tsp	cloves
1 tsp	black pepper corns
2	bay leaves
½ tsp	ground nutmeg
½ tsp	salt

Cook the chopped tomatoes, onions and garlic over a medium heat until soft, about 20 minutes. Strain through a kitchen sieve, and return to the pot. Add the remaining ingredients and bring to the boil. Reduce heat and cook until the sauce thickens. Strain through a sieve into sterilised bottles and seal.

Mayonnaise

2	fresh egg yolks
250ml	good quality sunflower oil
50ml	olive oil
1tblsp	Dijon mustard

Stir the mustard into the egg yolks and very slowly drizzle in the sunflower and olive oil, whisking as you pour. Care must be taken while you pour; if you go too fast you will get a curdled mess. Drizzle drop by drop. After you have poured in the first 100ml, you can start to drizzle a little faster. Keep going until all the oil is used up. Store in a clean jar.

Variation   Herb mayonnaise
Add 2 tblsp finely chopped herbs of choice to the finished mayonnaise. Chives are great on potato salad, dill and fennel add flavour to any fish dish.

Bouquet Garni

There are very few meat dishes in my repertoire that do not get adorned by a bouquet garni. I always make large ones and they should generally include bay, rosemary and thyme for red meat. You can also add sage or oregano as complementary flavours. For chicken, I replace the rosemary with sage and add fennel or parsley.

Basil & Almond Pesto

2	handfuls of basil
2	garlic cloves, peeled
50g	ground almonds
100g	grated parmesan
100ml	olive oil
	zest of 1 lemon

At the end of summer I collect all the basil leaves and make a huge batch of this pesto to freeze, leaving out the parmesan and almonds which I add as I use the defrosted mixture. Here is the recipe for enough to adorn a large bowl of pasta.

Place all the ingredients except the olive oil in the blender and blitz on the pulse setting. Be careful not to over-mix or you will get a mush. Drizzle in the olive oil and stir by hand. Serve. If you have time on your hands, tear the basil into a pestle and mortar, then add the garlic, stir in the other ingredients. I prefer the manual method if I'm making a small batch – you are less likely to over-chop, and the hand work is great therapy.

Herb & Chilli Jellies

2kg	apples
2kg	water
	white sugar
3	chillies (or more to taste)
10	blackberries (I use these for colour only, so they are optional, but it's nice to have a red jelly)

Chop the chillies and apples with peels and cores, add the berries, if you are using them, and simmer in the water until the apples are soft. Strain through a jelly bag or a sieve lined with a piece of muslin cloth into another large pot under the straining mixture. It will take at least 3 hours for the liquid you need to drip through. I leave it overnight to strain. Weigh the strained liquid and return to the heat. You will need the same amount of sugar as the liquid (i.e. 1 litre juice and 1kg sugar). Boil vigorously, stirring while the sugar dissolves. After this the liquid will clear as it boils. Allow to boil till it thickens, test by putting a spoon of the liquid on a saucer. Place in the fridge for 5 minutes and see if it crinkles when you push your finger through the setting jelly. Test often, as you don't want runny jelly but you also don't want a thick glob. When the jelly has thickened, pour into hot, sterilised jars and seal. The jelly will take 24 hours to set properly. If it is too runny, you can always boil it up some more and re-bottle.

Variation   For the herb jelly, replace the chilli and berries with 250ml chopped herbs of your choice per litre of liquid. Mint is my favourite, but you can experiment. Try placing a whole leaf or sprig of the herb in the clear jelly when you bottle it, so you can identify it later.

Lavender Jelly

Use half the amount of berries for a pink colour and replace the herbs with finely chopped lavender flowers.

Herb Butters

I always use these as a finishing touch for steaks or fish for added flavour. Mix some softened butter with finely chopped herbs. For 100g butter you will need a handful of finely chopped herbs. I use thyme and parsley most of the time, but have also used rosemary with lamb. You can roll the butter into a tube shape in clingfilm and store it in the fridge. This also freezes well.

Herb Oils

At the end of summer I always make a jar of basil oil; the plants die off for the winter, but their scent and flavour live on in the oil. You can make this with any herb, though. Into a full bottle of good quality olive oil, add a handful of clean, dry fresh basil leaves. Shake for a minute every couple of days for a week to infuse the flavours. After 2 weeks decant into a clean bottle and discard the leaves.

Herb Vinegars

As with the basil oil, I pick the last of my tarragon before the cold sets in. A handful of this I place in vinegar, to use in salad dressings throughout the winter months. Unlike the oils, the herbs can be left inside the vinegar.

Red Wine Vinaigrette

2 tblsp	red wine vinegar
120ml	good quality olive oil
2 tbsp	Dijon mustard
	salt & pepper

Pour all the ingredients into a clean jar, screw on the lid and shake. If you only have one
dressing, this has to be the one. The volumes below will generously dress a large salad,
but the trick is to double or treble the quantities so you have it ready next time.
It will keep for a couple of weeks in a sealed jar. All you have to do is shake it up and use.

Honey Mustard Dressing

120ml	good quality olive oil
2 tblsp	mayonnaise
1 tsp	wholegrain mustard
2 tblsp	white wine vinegar
1 tsp	honey
	salt & pepper

Like a good vinaigrette, you can use this very simple dressing to augment any salad
of fresh ingredients. It keeps in a jar in the fridge for only a week, though. Place all
the ingredients in a clean jar, screw on the lid and shake well to mix it. Every time you
use the dressing, just give it a good shake.

Herbs

You will have noticed the free hand I use with herbs in my recipes. I am a firm believer in the old adage about a kitchen garden being like an apothecary in the back yard. Herbs are good for you and allow you to season less and enjoy more subtle and complex flavours in your food. I'll often pick a large vase of herbs and place them instead of flowers in the kitchen; they look and smell good, and it saves dashing out in the rain in winter. They also help to keep flies at bay in the summer.

I'm probably as crazy about herbs as I am about tomatoes. I've been growing and cooking with them for as long as I can remember, only now I have the space to grow them in sack-loads. There's a little nursery for seedlings right outside the kitchen door and I plant them out almost from the door and throughout the kitchen garden. They are there as much for their culinary uses as companion plants for various crops. Depending on the species, they help control pests, augment flavour and bring marvellous aromas to the garden.

True to my nature, I produce far more herbs than I can possibly use. Although the various preserving techniques account for some of them, there is plenty of excess. Supplying to Wild Organics for their organic boxes is one way of using them up, but visitors rarely leave without a bunch of something fragrant from the garden.

Imbibe

Even though we practise mixed farming on Eikenbosch, in pursuit of our belief in organic living, the vine is the centre of economic activity here. Eikenbosch is a wine farm before anything else. We raise and tend and harvest our vines according to organic principles and make certified organic wine, much of which finds its way to the European market.

I love the process of making wine, if not for the wine itself, then for the balance and rhythm it brings to life. In summer there is great activity in the vineyards, checking the growth of the vine. Too many leaves affect the development of the fruit, too few affect how it ripens. I walk through the vineyard early each morning, among rows of lavender that form a blue haze where the bees are just waking up.

I invariably carry a basket to pick the melons, figs, beans and whatever else is ripe on my way to the vines. Closer to harvest time, and the daily sugar, taste and acid checks are the focus of these walks. Autumn brings the harvest, with tractors droning up and down and extra mouths to feed. In winter all activity transfers to the cellar. While stews and soups burble away on the stove, the wines are checked, racked and blended, awaiting the bottle.

This passing of the seasons, the ebb and flow of intense activity and periods of quiet anticipation, mark out the pace of our lives. Somehow it is all a little sweeter of an evening when there's a bottle of your own Chenin Blanc plunged into a bucket full of ice, just waiting to be shared and enjoyed.

List of Recipes